Leader, Draw Near

Devotions For Your Pursuit of God /

COL LARRY SIMPSON, USAF (Ret.)
with Bobbie Simpson

Scripture quotations marked NASB are taken from the New American Standard Bible®. Copyright © 1960, 1962, 1963, 1968, 1971, 1972, 1973, 1975, 1977, 1995 by The Lockman Foundation. Used by permission (www.Lockman.org).

Scripture quotations marked NKJV are taken from the New King James Version®. Copyright © 1982 by Thomas Nelson. Used by permission. All rights reserved.

Scripture quotations marked NIV are taken from The Holy Bible, New International Version®, NIV®. Copyright © 1973, 1978, 1984, 2011 by Biblica, Inc.® Used by permission. All rights reserved worldwide.

Scripture quotations marked ESV are from The Holy Bible, English Standard Version. Copyright © 2001 by Crossway Bibles, a publishing ministry of Good News Publishers.

Copyright © 2016 Officers' Christian Fellowship of the United States of America. All rights reserved. This book or parts thereof may not be reproduced in any form, stored in any retrieval system, or transmitted in any form by any means—electronic, mechanical, photocopy, recording, or otherwise—without prior written permission of the publisher, except as provided by United States of America copyright law.
For permission requests, write to the publisher at the address below.
Officers' Christian Fellowship
3784 S Inca Street
Englewood, CO 80110

ISBN-13:978-0-9979459-0-4

Acknowledgments

This effort would not have been possible without the tireless, loving support of my wife, Bobbie Simpson, who edited, provided endless encouragement, and helped give voice to many of these devotions. I am extremely grateful for her love and support.

I also want to thank the countless number of active duty military leaders I gathered with in early morning leader devotions, one-on-one discipleship and mentoring relationships.

To the many participants of Puget Sound Officers' Christian Fellowship Bible studies at Joint Base Lewis McChord, Naval Base Kitsap, Bremerton and Bangor, and Naval Air Station Whidbey Island, as well as many others who shared with me through email their triumphs and challenges in integrating faith and profession, I express my thanks.

Table of Contents

Acknowledgments v
Forward ix
How To Use This Devotional xi
Whose heart has God touched? xi

53 WEEKLY DEVOTIONALS
The Leader and Mercy 3
Righteous Living and The Righteous Leader 5
Double Portion 7
Faithful Leadership 9
Monthly Reflection 12

Undivided Heart 15
Don't Work Alone! Enlist & Mentor 17
Was It Failure or Success? 19
Truth and The Christian Leader 21
Question Authority 23
Monthly Reflection 26

Any Volunteers? 29
Battle Rhythm 31
Reality Check 33
A Firm Foundation 35
Monthly Reflection 38

Satisfaction 41
Compliant Clay 43
Practice Makes Perfect 45
Reignited Service 47
An Actionable Plan 49
Monthly Reflection 52

Faith Rhythm	55
Big-Picture Perspective	57
Commander's Intent	59
Lasting Influence	61
Monthly Reflection	64
What Say Ye?	67
Are You Leading?	69
Your Every Need	71
Loyalty	73
What Do You Want From Me?	75
Monthly Reflection	78
Let Us Go	81
A Soldier's Memorial	83
Strengthen Yourself	85
Condition of Service	87
Monthly Reflection	90
Restoration	93
Himself for Me	95
Justice, Mercy & Humility	97
Desired End State	99
Ready or Not	101
Monthly Reflection	104
Nagging Circumstances	107
Distractions	109
In His Time	111
The Way Ahead—Choose to Forgive	113
Monthly Reflection	116

Unintended Consequences	119
The Preeminent God	121
Seeing the Other Side	123
Compassion	125
Did You Ask?	127
Monthly Reflection	130
Transformation: Clean the Root and Reinsert It	133
The Right Heart	135
Daniel's Wise Alternative	137
Character of a Leader—Holy?	139
Monthly Reflection	142
Discouragement—I Have Had Enough!	145
Where Now is the Lord?	147
Rest Interrupted—Reasonable Work/Rest Rhythm	149
He Will Be With You	151
Monthly Reflection	154
About OCF	159

Forward

This devotional has been a work of love in development for the past couple of years through close-quarter ministry with countless leaders this ministry touches every day.

Larry Simpson has poured his heart into writing these devotions to challenge leaders to live out Christ's example in their work, homes, ministries, and arenas of influence. The writings of this devotional have personally "ministered to me where I needed it." I know they will do the same for you.

This is not a five-minute manager devotional, as beneficial as five minutes every day in the Word can be. This is a devotional designed to encourage readers to move through at their own pace, trusting the Spirit to give insight that transforms. The intent is that you will spend time looking up and reflecting on Scripture references and that you will allow God to touch your heart as you meditate on the thoughts and challenges of each devotion—and in particular, the monthly reflection sections.

I encourage you to engage each reading and to walk through it with a friend, a small group of leaders, a "battle buddy," or in a mentoring relationship. I am confident that *Leader, Draw Near* will have a life encouragement impact on each person who reads it.

David B. Warner, Brig Gen, USAF (Ret.)
Executive Director, Officers' Christian Fellowship

Introduction

How To Use This Devotional

Welcome to *Leader Draw Near: Devotions For Your Pursuit of God*. Who is a leader? You—the one who turns to God for wisdom and direction in leading others.

This book is designed as a year of weekly devotions. Each devotional is fashioned to prompt reflection on a specific topic. Readers are encouraged to search out each Scripture reference and to lean into God for more light as He meets you where you are. Each reading offers Points to Ponder, geared for that specific intent.

Every 4-5 weeks, I have included a monthly reflection sheet. These monthly reflection sheets may or may not correspond directly to a calendar month, but that's OK—these sheets are designed to help you gauge your habit of integrating faith and profession, and they will also help get you into the habit of keeping a written record of those times when the Holy Spirit speaks to you. I encourage you to engage each topic throughout the week and to list personal reflections and applications as God touches your heart.

Whose heart has God touched?

"But it is not this way with you; but the one who is the greatest among you must become like the youngest, and the leader like the servant" (Luke 22:26, NASB).

A consistent pursuit of God will help the Christian leader honor God, serve others, and fulfill one's leadership responsibilities. Leadership is about performance and meeting mission requirements in a positive and fruitful way. The leader who intentionally integrates the teachings of Scripture into daily decision making will have lasting influence and will lead with integrity, humility and a servant's heart.

The heart can be upright and the possessor full of rejoicing. Indeed, he shouts with joy (Psalm 32:11). How can the heart avoid wickedness and become a wellspring of encouragement, boldness, and wisdom? Jesus does not ask leaders to shed self dignity, nor does He ask us to forfeit intellect, emotional passion, or drive in order to gain the title of servant leader.

Christ would have one lead with godliness and a servant's heart. True servant leadership is other focused. At the heart of decisions, Christ can be found. When asked to disclose the greatest command, His answer was "love." When asked which of the disciples was the greatest, He announced, the one who leads like a servant.

Many of the devotions in this book were written following weekly devotional interaction with active duty military officers and NCOs. Some of the comments and Points to Ponder reflect the hearts and daily efforts of military leaders (officers and enlisted) who strive to live out their faith in the military and in all they do.

My hope and prayer is that these devotionals will help you enter into a time of self reflection, encouragement, and spiritual transformation as you draw near to God. May He grant that these devotional thoughts fill you with the love and mind of Christ in your pursuit of God.

Leader, Draw Near

Devotions For Your Pursuit of God /

53 Weekly Devotions for Leaders

01 /

The Leader and Mercy

"Shouldn't you have had mercy on your fellow servant just as I had on you?" (Matthew 18:33, NIV).

Yes—but what about the consequences? As Christ followers one of the questions we must consider is "Do we find it hard to show mercy?" In striving to live out one's faith in one's profession, Christian leaders must rightly handle this issue. In Matthew 18:21-35 the apostle Peter asked Jesus for clarification as to how often he must forgive a fellow believer who sins against him. In leadership this is not a rhetorical question. Apparently, Peter's personal or leadership experience had presented him with the brother who made a habit of offending others, taking advantage them, or evading responsibility.

Understandably, hypocrisy is a label believers deserve if we display the response of the merciless servant referred to in Matthew 18:33, but what about consequences for certain actions and our requirement to hold others accountable? With authority comes responsibility to maintain standards and acceptable levels of performance. The leader basically bears the responsibility to correct, discipline and keep communication channels open. He or she is also accountable to foster goodwill and to forgive.

Though not exclusively a leadership problem, Christ demonstrates the correct response to be the practice of mercy, compassion, or forgiveness. Christ does not limit the number of times one is to forgive because His action on the cross would provide the most lavish, inclusive display the world would ever witness. So great and undeserved would be the forgiveness He grants that through Peter we are warned of the severe consequences of refusing to forgive. If you find it hard to forgive, remember that we were all once in need of underserved grace and were shown mercy (1 Peter 2:25).

POINTS TO PONDER

> In the home or at work, would our response to offenders be different if we asked ourselves, "What would Jesus do?" (Matthew 18:33).

> The king in the account had an expectation of the servant he forgave. In our deliberations will we consider the positive change forgiveness can bring about in an offender's life? (2 Corinthians 2:7).

> Regardless of another's response to our leniency, what effect will our willingness to be merciful have on our own character and quality of life? (Matthew 18:35).

02 /

Righteous Living and The Righteous Leader

"And having been freed from sin, you became slaves of righteousness" (Romans 6:18, NASB).

By what do we choose to be mastered? Men and women who have committed to serve in the military might easily, if jokingly, identify the military as their master. Do Christian military personnel see this in a different light?

The entire discourse of Romans 6 is a liberating reminder that righteous living is part and parcel of salvation. Christian leaders cannot pursue both sin and righteous living. We must choose our master. Honestly, who would willingly be enslaved to anything? Yet, slaves we are to the voice we heed and the conduct we perform.

A well-known scholar quipped, "People must be charmed into righteousness." Was Job charmed into righteousness? Satan mistakenly believed that God had allured Job into faithful obedience and blameless integrity. Even Job's wife believed that God's failure to protect his family and possessions were grounds for Job to "curse God and die" (Job 2:9).

Job's intimate friendship with God had made a new man of Job. He cared for widows, the blind and lame, the needy, the stranger, even the dying. Righteousness and justice were his clothing. Even in testing and loss, Job worshipped God (Job 1:20-21) and spoke the truth about God (Job 42:8). Righteous living is the compelling response to fellowship with God.

This brings me to my second thought. How do we as "righteous" leaders live out righteousness in the workplace? Thinking rightly about God puts leaders in a better position to do right. Job had shut the door on thinking or doing evil and had become a slave to righteousness (Job 2:3). He was free to live a noteworthy life free of compromise, even in devastating circumstances. His testimony to us is one of perseverance in the things of God in every situation. As we practice righteousness, righteousness will become our nature, just as Christ is righteous (1 John 3:7). Leaders, may others follow your lead as you are mastered by right living.

POINTS TO PONDER

> Are we tempted to compromise our Christian ethic and do what's expedient (even if it's wrong) to benefit from a deal that is too good to pass up? (Nehemiah 5:15).

> Are we careful to maintain godly righteousness in the face of shifting priorities and requirements? (1 Samuel 13:11-12).

> Are we measuring ourselves according to the standards of Christian righteousness and Romans 6:18?

03 /
Double Portion

"And so it was, when they had crossed over, that Elijah said to Elisha, 'Ask! What may I do for you, before I am taken away from you?' Elisha said, 'Please let a double portion of your spirit be upon me'" (2 Kings 2:9, NKJV).

Great leaders are not satisfied with the status quo or content with mediocre gains. As a leader in the home and workplace, how comfortable are you in asking God for big things?

Elisha's request prompts me to ask myself: How far am I willing to go with God? Elijah's successor was willing to go all the way and beyond.

As it relates to Christian leadership, much can be gleaned from Elisha's request for "a double portion." First, Elisha's bold request reminds me that God always has a plan for the continuance of His divine mission. Elisha asked for what the successor or inheritor was due. In asking and receiving, Elisha's legitimate claim was established. With his master's cloak, he immediately performed miracles in keeping with the authority of one who would speak for God. The need for convincing, authentic leadership is as important today as it was in Elisha's day (2 Chronicles 16:9a). Through leaders like Elisha, Asa, and Jeremiah, leaders are challenged to call on God who will reveal His plan (Jeremiah 33:3) and His way.

Second, God's work does not cease with key personnel turnover. Moses led Israel out of captivity, but it was Joshua who led them into the Promised Land. Likewise, David had a desire for a temple dedicated to God, but it was Solomon who built it. Also, various kings before Asa did not remove idols from the land, but Asa, king of Judah "took courage and removed the abominable idols" (2 Chronicles 15:8). We cannot put God in a box regarding the who, when, or where of His unchanging plan.

As you consider Elisha's request, does it rise up in you, as it does in me, to avoid using expressions such as "indispensable and irreplaceable" when it comes to turnover in personnel or volunteers? Completion of God's mission is not up for grabs nor is it personality dependent. God's mission is enduring. We, as leaders, might consider asking Him to provide replacements that possess a "double portion" to help carry out the mission He has given us to do.

POINTS TO PONDER

> What ministry, project, or relationship will you trust God to take to the next level? (Psalm 90:17; Proverbs 19:21).

> What steps are you taking to equip another for the important work you are currently doing? (2 Timothy 2:2-4, 15-16).

> If someone asked for a double portion of your spirit, what would they be asking for? (Ephesians 4:20-24; 5:1).

04 /
Faithful Leadership

"And you know in all your hearts and in all your souls that not one thing has failed of all the good things which the LORD your God spoke concerning you. All have come to pass for you; not one word of them has failed" (Joshua 23:14, NKJV).

Read the verse again, but this time more slowly. What stood out to you? For me it is the phrase: "Not one word of them has failed."

Joshua's declaration is riveting. God's promises were to Abraham, Isaac, and Jacob initially and later to Moses and Joshua (Joshua 24:1-5) and had covered countless miles of journeying and hundreds of years. Amazingly, not one promise of protection and deliverance had failed. Since God has demonstrated such faithfulness, Joshua is challenging the Israelites to consider not endangering their own well being by failing to love and obey the Lord their God.

From a leadership perspective, I must ask: What enables Christian leaders to maintain the charge when all around us say, "Give up?" Oaths, contracts, and legal agreements bind some to the task, but that which binds the Christian and Christian leader is God's demonstrated faithfulness. Have you, like Joshua's audience, chronicled the trustworthiness of God in your journey? Joshua spoke confidently of what they had seen and knew about God's fidelity. A reading of Joshua 23 and 24 reveals a strikingly impressive history of God's providence over his people. As you look back, are you struck by the consistency of God's work on your behalf?

POINTS TO PONDER

If you are given to 20/20 hindsight, as I am, examine your leadership through these lenses:

> Do you have the assurance that you are part of God's master plan? (Jeremiah 29:11-13).

> On a daily basis, can you rest confidently knowing that He will come through (again) in unexpected ways? (Matthew 6:33-34; Philippians 4:19).

> Will you abandon the "failure prevent" mode of performance and perform "heartily as for the Lord rather than for men?" (Colossians 3:23).

> Is your daily allegiance to and trust in God commensurate with His faithfulness to you? (1 John 4:19; Romans 5:8).

Monthly Reflection

Monthly Reflection

It's time for a quick evaluation. Use this section to help gauge your habit of integrating faith and profession, and to help get you into the habit of keeping a written record of those times when the Holy Spirit speaks to you. Use the questions below for monthly reflection and to aid a spiritual approach to challenges confronting your application of faith and leadership. The questions are intended for the purpose of self-reflection and contemplation—not guilt and self-loathing.

1. Among your daily requirements, were you able to achieve aside time with God through personal reading of Scripture and prayer?

☐ Yes
☐ No

2. Recall one or two of the most significant leadership challenges you encountered over the past 30 days. What was your response to the challenge(s) and what effect, if any, did your spiritual development priority have on how you addressed the situation?

_____
_____
_____
_____
_____
_____
_____
_____
_____
_____

3. Reflecting over the past 30 days, name one or two ways you met balance between work and family requirements.

4. Have you recently observed an event that you would count as answered prayer?

☐ Yes (explain)

☐ No

5. Did you enlist the aid of a prayer partner over the last 30 days?

☐ Yes
☐ No

05 /
Undivided Heart

"Teach me your way, O LORD, and I will walk in your truth; give me an undivided heart, that I may fear your name" (Psalm 86:11*).

As a leader, are you ever hesitant or uncertain about how to respond to situations? Are you inclined to give a knee-jerk reaction or are your responses more often guided by the Lord's true wisdom? Do you experience compassion level fluctuations, that is, sometimes your actions reflect spiritual wisdom and at other times seem void of anything resembling those guided by the Holy Spirit? At the heart of these queries is the consideration of the root of one's conscious choices or actions. Our options are to allow the "spiritual self" or to allow the "old nature" to dictate decisions.

David's prayer is a rejection of the old self. Left to his own devices or contemplations, David, like many of us, could find himself poised to make poor decisions with disastrous consequences (2 Samuel 11). No, David's desire is to be taught God's truth so that more and more he would walk in God's ways. He resisted having a divided heart. David's default in times of struggle was to walk in God's truth. Is it possible to discern right judgment without knowing the Truth? James 1:8 reads, "A double minded man is unstable in all his ways." Surely, as Christian leaders, our desire is to show compassion with an undivided heart—one that rightly discerns truth with reverence for the Lord.

POINTS TO PONDER

As you read the Bible and especially contemplate Psalm 86:11, consider these simple action points:

> Act according to revealed truth, recognizing that spiritual leadership is dynamic.

> Be sensitive to what the Lord is teaching.

> Practice putting God's plan into action, daily.

* *"The Living Insights Study Bible,"* General Editor, Charles Swindoll, 1996, (NIV).

> Faith, mobilized in our daily leadership actions, finds expression in Oswald Chambers' statement: "Faith is the indefinable certainty of God behind everything, and is the one thing that the Spirit of God makes clearer and clearer as we go on."

06 /

Don't Work Alone! Enlist & Mentor

"So when Moses' father-in-law saw all that he did for the people, he said, 'What is this thing that you are doing for the people? Why do you alone sit, and all the people stand before you from morning until evening?'" (Exodus 18:14, NKJV).

Jethro's question commands a response. Think on it. Moses, whose face glowed because of his close presence to God, is being told, "The thing that you are doing is not good" (Exodus 18:17). That is the last thing a leader wants to hear, especially one who had just led over a million people from slavery to freedom! Read the entire account. Moses was painstakingly judging disputes "between a man and his neighbor" (Exodus 18:16) and individually explaining the ordinances of God. Talking about being in the weeds! Moses, Israel's new national leader, was in the weeds trying to fix disputes over who knows what when his father-in-law asks this striking query.

What brings leaders to the point of task overload—the belief that only we know what's best, perhaps distrust of others, or possibly personal ownership? Moses' knowledge or wisdom was to be for the good of the entire people—not just for individual cases. The dispensing of judgments should not have come at the expense of his health or of exhaustion. Reading Exodus 18:14-26 helps put a few thoughts in order. The passage provokes a pause, an examination, and a reordering of priorities.

How are you doing in your pursuit to invite others with similar heart and vision (Exodus 18:21) into your area of responsibility? It has been stated: "We must exercise wisdom and discernment and desire God's model" to meet the task at hand. Sometimes ours is to help others understand their spiritual gift and put it to use. Begin to take notice of those with similar conviction and compassion who are able to live out God's model for a shared burden of leadership.

There is another leadership quality we can take away from our review of Jethro's counsel. Jethro explained his rationale to Moses. Leaders mentor when they take time to explain their decisions. I so admire Moses' humility and respect for his father-in-law (Exodus 18:24), and I love the spirit of Jethro's counsel: "I will give you counsel and God will be with you" (Exodus 18:19).

POINTS TO PONDER

> Leadership recognizes needs and addresses them through the skills and talents of like minded people.

> Search for and desire God's response to fulfilling needs. Ask God to bring people in your life, such as a Jethro, who have your best interest in mind.

> Humbly receive God's guidance.

07 /

Was It Failure or Success?

"But Simon answered and said to Him, 'Master, we have toiled all night and caught nothing; nevertheless at Your word I will let down the net'" (Luke 5:5, NKJV).

To me, Luke 5:5 is a curious object lesson. On the one hand, Peter, a skilled fisherman, could have been insulted that Jesus asked him to demonstrate once more what he had repeatedly failed at throughout the day. On the other hand, Jesus allowed him the opportunity to demonstrate faith and trust.

One might ask: Did Simon really fail, or was his unproductive fishing day tied to Christ's master plan and call? I would think the latter. How might we apply Peter's object lessons to our own situations?

POINTS TO PONDER

> Recognize that God has a master plan. Failure is a part of living. As leaders, however, we have the ability to serve as change agents—and what agents for change we can be! Having been bounced around from shop to shop, a young sergeant once said to me, "Someone must give me a chance at some point." Christ gives us occasion after occasion to demonstrate faith in His ability to make our lives productive.

> Demonstrate active concern. Christian leaders have an opportunity to help others live productive lives. Ultimately, we become a part of God's eternal plan in the lives of others. Although God's ways are not always easy to discern, He is still in the instruction business. Patient persistence and courage are effective stabilizers when faced with unrealistic alternatives.

> God can use us! In spite of our flux and failures, do not be afraid to approach Him or feel unworthy of His use. A temporal failure does not have to be permanent.

Be full of courage (Joshua 1:9). At the Master's command, try again. He has an awesome plan for you (Luke 5:8-10) even when things may not seem to flow logically.

> "Nevertheless at Your word I will let down the net." In the face of failure, Simon did not give up. His was not a blind faith. He trusted Jesus for the things he had already seen Him do. What about you? Have you backed away from a challenge because the results have been slow to come? Remember, in God's economy there is no waste. "All things work together for good..."

08 /

Truth and The Christian Leader

"Then Ananias, hearing these words, fell down and breathed his last. So great fear came upon all those who heard these things" (Acts 5:5, NKJV).

A close reading of Acts 5:1-11, the account of Ananias and Sapphira's deceit, should lead one to conclude that truth is the essential thing. In this perplexing story, which takes place as the early church was forming, maintaining a standard of truth and honesty proved to be the bedrock for the church and our Christian faith. Those endowed with leadership responsibility needed to set and safeguard ethical standards. Many are shocked at the decisive, harsh response to the couple's duplicity, yet neither Peter nor the disciples brought about the speedy demise of this couple. They lied to the Spirit of the Lord.

How might the Christian leader apply the lesson of Ananias and Sapphira in the work place? I can recall saying or hearing others say: "I have to make an example of this one." Why is it necessary for a leader to take extreme positions?

The practice of truth and maintaining high standards is paramount for the Christian leader. The leader often finds himself or herself in a position to judge matters that have lasting import for the individual, the unit, perhaps the family, and others. In 2 Timothy 2:15 Paul encourages diligence, which leads to right decisions and honorable handling of truth. Essentially, practicing truth helps one hold a straight course with an integrity that withstands scrutiny. Requiring integrity in those one leads sets the stage for marketplace and home effectiveness and stability.

Pilate said to Jesus in John 18:38, "What is truth?" Truth is the foundation on which we stand and is what Christian leaders are called to practice.

POINTS TO PONDER

> The Christian leader who upholds truth protects the integrity of institutions established by God.

> The Christian leader sends a compelling message to others to "put away lying" and to speak truth to every man (Ephesians 4:25).

> The Christian leader, as Peter modeled, would do well to allow all involved a chance to tell his/her side of the story. Audi Alteram Partem cautions us to hear the other side. Leaders need not fear truth but must pursue it.

09 /

Question Authority

"Then the LORD answered Job out of the whirlwind, and said: 'Who is this who darkens counsel by words without knowledge? Now prepare yourself like a man; I will question you, and you shall answer Me'"
(Job 38:1-3, NKJV).

From my experience, most leaders don't care to have their decisions challenged. This is particularly true when the pace is fast and compliance must be immediate. In reference to this Job passage a leader observed, "There are some things you are not supposed to understand." This was certainly the case with Job. For all of Job's righteousness, one might question whether Job deserved to suffer and, if he did, should he at least have been given insight as to why.

As we strive to live out our faith in our profession, the study of Job prompts a few thoughts to consider: Can we approach God with high emotions when circumstances demand justice? In a vacuum of discernment of how God is working, can we question the fairness of what He allows? What should our response be to trials we do not understand? Job's response was to question God. One might conclude that Job got wrapped up in matters too great for him. As leaders, we often consider the big picture, the larger plan.

Oftentimes, the big picture does not get translated down through the working level. In a similar way, a far greater reality than our own exists in the heavenly economy. As God cross examined Job (read Job chapters 38-41), revealing Job's lack of knowledge of His creation and of His divine power, Job's only response was: "Behold I am insignificant; what can I reply to you? I lay my hand on my mouth" (Job 40:4). Job finally got it.

In the workplace we are not always privy to the larger plan. We may be in the dark, not knowing how or whether we have a role to play. It can also be that way in God's greater scheme. What we do know is that God is

Lord and ruler over all. His ways are unsearchable; they defy humanity's thoughts and wisdom.

So should we question God's authority? Regardless of how righteous the question might seem, of how strongly I might feel about an injustice, or of how merciful I think God should be, I would be wise to consider the Holy Scriptures and to pattern my questions and concerns after Jesus' response while here on earth.

POINTS TO PONDER

> Pray. When Jesus was anxious, He prayed (Mark 14:34).

> Desire God's will (Mark 14:36).

> Rest confidently in Him (John 11:41b-42).

I had a friend who, in response to matters he did not understand or was reluctant to accept, would say: "I am content to leave this in the hands of a sovereign God." What a great response! As we walk and lead by faith, fulfilling God's mission, may we entrust our ways and life's circumstances to Him.

Monthly Reflection

Monthly Reflection

It's time for a quick evaluation. Use this section to help gauge your habit of integrating faith and profession, and to help get you into the habit of keeping a written record of those times when the Holy Spirit speaks to you. Use the questions below for monthly reflection and to aid a spiritual approach to challenges confronting your application of faith and leadership. The questions are intended for the purpose of self-reflection and contemplation—not guilt and self-loathing.

1. Among your daily requirements, were you able to achieve aside time with God through personal reading of Scripture and prayer?

☐ Yes
☐ No

2. Recall one or two of the most significant leadership challenges you encountered over the past 30 days. What was your response to the challenge(s) and what effect, if any, did your spiritual development priority have on how you addressed the situation?

_____
_____
_____
_____
_____
_____
_____
_____
_____
_____

3. Reflecting over the past 30 days, name one or two ways you met balance between work and family requirements.

_____
_____
_____
_____
_____
_____
_____
_____
_____
_____
_____
_____

4. Have you recently observed an event that you would count as answered prayer?

☐ Yes (explain) _____
_____

☐ No

5. Did you enlist the aid of a prayer partner over the last 30 days?

☐ Yes
☐ No

10 /
Any Volunteers?

"Let no one despise your youth, but be an example to the believers in word, in conduct, in love, in spirit, in faith, in purity" (1 Timothy 4:12, NKJV).

"We need a volunteer." During a small group, morning devotion time, one of the guys commented, what if Paul had said instead: "We need a volunteer?" Do you think Timothy would have stepped forward? That question reflects good insight into the instructions Paul gives Timothy. Read the entirety of 1 Timothy 4 for a more complete grasp of the issues and of Paul's admonitions.

Paul was wise enough not to give Timothy the idea that he was serving as a volunteer. Taught by his grandmother Lois and his mother Eunice (2 Timothy 1:5), Timothy had been prepared for the call early in his life. Later, Paul calls him "his true son in the faith," and we see Timothy being mentored in the hard work of an evangelist called to plant and strengthen churches, much as Paul and the other apostles were doing. Fittingly, Paul speaks to Timothy as a wise mentor, tutor, and encourager. The entire chapter aptly captures the confidence Paul instilled in Timothy. Essentially, Paul was saying to Timothy, "Live out what you believe and let others see you doing it."

Who can live without encouragement? I am not referring to the light pat on the back that comes with completion of a physical fitness test or from a cheering crowd of observers watching you stride to the finish line at the end of a 5K, or even from the congratulations that accompany a well-deserved promotion. Those are all good things! I am talking about the encouragement that comes from one who is fully vested in your daily walk with the Lord.

As leaders and mentors, what mentorship lessons might we take from Paul in his heartfelt concern for Timothy?

POINTS TO PONDER

> Instill confidence in what they are doing, perseverance to the calling, and modeling a life worthy of emulation. They must encourage others to live out their calling—even when it gets tough (1 Timothy 4:11, 12, 14).

> Express loving, yet genuine, in-your-face concern. Encourage your Timothy to wrestle, struggle, and endure. Express a "do whatever it takes" commitment to see a task through and live out what he or she knows the Lord has called them to do (1 Timothy 4:15).

> Capture and remove ambiguity. Confirm the path of the one being mentored with gentle reminders that his or her efforts are also for the good of others (1 Timothy 4:16).

Who around you needs your tutelage and encouragement? Let's imitate what Paul did for Timothy. Don't ask for volunteers, but encourage others to fulfill their calling or act of service.

11 /
Battle Rhythm

"But Martha was distracted with all her preparations; and she came up to Him and said, 'Lord, do You not care that my sister has left me to do all the serving alone? Then tell her to help me'" (Luke 10:40, NASB).

Martha asked Jesus to tell Mary (her sister) to help her in the flurry of preparation that accompanies preparing for guests. This Scripture prompts important questions for consideration: When do you surge and go all out to achieve a task? When should you pull back for contemplation, admiration, appreciation or just rest? However you respond to those questions, Mary's action, "…Seated at the Lord's feet, listening to His word" (Luke 10:39), presents an important consideration as we go about our busy lives and full schedules.

For me, a fine line exists between activity and my spiritual act of service. I would like to think that everything I do is a by-product of the service I offer the Lord. Well, not so fast. As someone once said: "When your activity consumes your time and energies so that you have no time for Him, you have become too busy!"

How are you doing when it comes to sorting through the competing priorities in your life? What's your battle rhythm? The one who goes all out but fails to recognize appropriate times to slow the surge and experience the presence of the Lord might be exhibiting the "Martha, Martha" syndrome. Read Jesus' gentle yet pointed response to Martha's request: "Martha, Martha, you are worried and bothered about so many things; but only one thing is necessary, for Mary has chosen the good part, which shall not be taken away from her" (Luke 10:41-42).

POINTS TO PONDER

> A leader's daily activities are wrapped in priorities, and it is essential to make the

right choice at the right time. Mary knew when to busy herself and when to be still. What about you? When you go into the Lord's presence, do you sit patiently at His feet in admiration of Him?

> Are you able to turn off or adjust your battle rhythm for the renewal and restoration that only comes from being in His presence? Jesus placed a premium on unhurried time and rest with Him.

> Mary got it right. She pulled back and gave her full, undivided time and attention to the One worthy of her total admiration—even at the risk of disappointing someone who was counting on her. We would do well to follow Mary's lead, which would make us less likely to overlook the people and things that really matter.

12 /
Reality Check

"This is the word of the LORD to Zerubbabel saying, 'Not by might nor by power, but by My Spirit,' says the LORD of hosts" (Zechariah 4:6, NASB).

Leaders, in our zeal to do and accomplish, how closely do we follow God's divine guidance? Yes, we should have passion for our work, and we should thrive to do things in community with others. Read Zechariah 4:1-14. In context, Joshua the priest and Zerubbabel the governor are likely the two anointed ones who stand by the Lord. Returning home after seventy years, the formerly exiled children of Israel desired to see the temple rebuilt. As far as Israel was concerned, restoration of the temple was job one, a goal which the governmental heads and the spiritual leadership were willing to cooperate to achieve.

Despite man's best intentions and even focused passion, we are reminded that God has a divine perspective: "Not by might nor by power, but by My Spirit." So where do we, in our leadership zeal, draw the line when it comes to pushing our own agenda or totally acquiescing to God's divine plan? Are we convinced that God has a plan, or do we "head fake" God by developing our plan then devoutly asking His blessing. The Lord's comment to Zechariah gives me pause to consider my motives in service. Consider the following as we purpose to serve God on His terms.

POINTS TO PONDER

> Prayerfully distinguish your will from the Father's will then quickly close the door on your fleshly desire. Model Jesus' prayer: "Nevertheless not my will, but thine be done" (Luke 22:42b). Every good plan is not God's plan.

> Desire the temple not built by human hands. "Or do you not know that your body is the temple of the Holy Spirit who is in you, whom you have from God, and that you are not your own?" (1 Corinthians 6:19, NASB). Through His Spirit, the Father

guides our actions, equipping us to live out our purpose to His glory. Ask God to help you maintain sight and respect for His temple so that you will be fitted for noble, eternal purposes.

> Worship God appropriately. May our service in His name be a spiritual act of worship. In doing so, when the Lord redirects our zealous labor, we will be at complete peace with His action(s).

13 /

A Firm Foundation

"Therefore everyone who hears these words of Mine and acts on them, may be compared to a wise man who built his house on the rock" (Matthew 7:24, NASB).

I have to think that deep down inside most of us typically have a sense of how to respond to adversity and challenging circumstances. So the question isn't what should I do, but how will I choose to respond? Will I succumb to the demands of the event or will my response come forth from the foundation of my sum total of spiritual development?

Jesus said that everyone who hears and acts on His words is wise. That wise one will be the person all eyes turn to in the midst of tragedy and need. His or her response will generally tell all. "The rain fell, and the floods came, and the winds blew and slammed against that house; and yet it did not fall, for it had been founded on the rock" (Matthew 7:25). Often, it is not the tragedy that determines the strength of our spiritual foundation; it is the aftereffects. The strength of our building materials will be revealed in how our life of faith is lived out. In the leader's case, how we walk in view and out of view of the public's eye will speak volumes about what we truly believe and the source of our strength.

It has been said, "There are no shortcuts to spiritual maturity." For the believer, the culmination of life changing experiences, hammered out through systematic, daily practices, produces maturity. This growth is undergirded by implementing God's truths and by adding layer upon layer of foundational servant leadership. When I was a child, we played a game called "Follow the Leader." As an adult, it is not a game. The world is watching, and those in our sphere of influence will follow our lead.

Consider Jesus' words: "Everyone who hears these words of mine and does not act on them will be like a foolish man who built his house on the sand"

(Matthew 7:26). In these days of rapid fire media and handheld media devices, word travels fast. The servant leader's challenge is to display a Christ like response when life changing moments arise, and thus be seen as the "wise man" with a firm foundation. Consider these practices of one who strives daily to live a foundational servant leader lifestyle.

POINTS TO PONDER

The Servant Leader...
> Acts on the teachings of Scripture and helps others do likewise.

> Models biblical living and lives out his/her faith wisely in front of others (Matthew 7:24).

> Serves as a ready testimony, realizing that he can do nothing apart from Christ (Philippians 4:13).

> Displays faithful actions that enable one to withstand the potentially destructive effects of adversity (Matthew 7:25).

Monthly Reflection

Monthly Reflection

It's time for a quick evaluation. Use this section to help gauge your habit of integrating faith and profession, and to help get you into the habit of keeping a written record of those times when the Holy Spirit speaks to you. Use the questions below for monthly reflection and to aid a spiritual approach to challenges confronting your application of faith and leadership. The questions are intended for the purpose of self-reflection and contemplation—not guilt and self-loathing.

1. Among your daily requirements, were you able to achieve aside time with God through personal reading of Scripture and prayer?

☐ Yes
☐ No

2. Recall one or two of the most significant leadership challenges you encountered over the past 30 days. What was your response to the challenge(s) and what effect, if any, did your spiritual development priority have on how you addressed the situation?

_____
_____
_____
_____
_____
_____
_____
_____
_____
_____
_____

3. Reflecting over the past 30 days, name one or two ways you met balance between work and family requirements.

_____
_____
_____
_____
_____
_____
_____
_____
_____
_____
_____
_____

4. Have you recently observed an event that you would count as answered prayer?

☐ Yes (explain) _____
_____

☐ No

5. Did you enlist the aid of a prayer partner over the last 30 days?

☐ Yes
☐ No

14 /
Satisfaction

"Jesus said to them, 'My food is to do the will of Him who sent Me and to accomplish His work'" (John 4:34, NASB).

What happens when the Christian leader stays true to the task and maintains focus despite signs of indifference and rejection? He finds satisfaction in a job well done and his efforts benefit those he is called to serve. From a close reading of John 4:7-42, one might conclude that the courageous leader who stays to the task ultimately helps others become better people.

The Samaritan woman received salvation, a regenerated life. Through her newfound faith, she pointed many others to Jesus. When they heard for themselves, they believed that Christ was "indeed the Savior of the world" (John 4:39-42). The leader bridges cultural divides and finds satisfaction when he/she does not quit at signs of rejection. The woman at the well was a Samaritan and Jesus, Jewish. Historically, the two ethnic groups did not interact. Not only could Jesus have rejected the woman, she could have also rejected Him and refused what He had to offer (John 4:9, 20, 22, 27).

POINTS TO PONDER

> The leader keeps a frontal awareness of why he is doing what he is called to do. Jesus persisted in his offer: "If you knew the gift of God, and who it is who says to you 'Give me a drink,' you would have asked Him, and He would have given you living water" (John 4:10). Not offended, nor hardened by rejection, the leader keeps to the task.

> The leader removes barriers for the good of the one in need. Jesus gave the woman the opportunity to confess her past mistakes (John 4:16-18). He did so without assigning condemnation or judgment.

> The leader's satisfaction comes in doing what he is called to do. When the disciples offered Jesus food, Jesus had no appetite for what satisfies the flesh. His satisfaction had come in engaging this marginalized outsider and in crossing cultural barriers in the name of the Father and for the sake of a race of people who needed the message of salvation. The result was marvelous! Many Samaritans believed (John 4:39-42). Jesus did not vacate the area or seek a transfer; He actually went out of His way to encounter her. He modeled what a good leader does…He made himself fully available, spoke truth in love, spent time with the people and saw lives changed.

Jesus was so committed to His service that, metaphorically, it served as His physical nourishment. What about you? Does your stalwart service satisfy you as nourishment. Remember the words of Paul. "Whatever you do, do your work heartily as for the Lord rather than for men" (Colossians 3:23). Let your selfless service be your satisfaction and nourishment.

15 /

Compliant Clay

"'Can I not, O house of Israel, deal with you as this potter does?' declares the LORD. 'Behold, like the clay in the potter's hand, so are you in My hand, O house of Israel'" (Jeremiah 18:6, NASB).

How do you respond to shaping? I mean the kind of shaping that causes you to conform fully to the one doing the shaping. Some of us conform better than others. As leaders, do you reflect the positive image you desire to see in your followers?

"Behold, like the clay in the potter's hand, so are you in My hand." When the potter is satisfied with his work, he displays it for use and admiration. The potter only reshapes the clay when the clay fails to conform to the image the potter intends to fashion. My heart's cry is to be a vessel fitted for His purposes. If that necessitates reshaping, I am in the faithful potter's hand.

So it is with the believer. Jesus declared, "You did not choose Me but I chose you..." (John 15:16). God calls us for specific purposes and each purpose comes with an expectation. Though God may deal with us (the clay) as He pleases, we need not be anxious or apprehensive of His molding as we present ourselves to Him in total submission to His skillful hand (Psalm 78:72).

What behavior might warrant reshaping? "Now the deeds of the flesh are evident, which are: immorality, impurity, sensuality, idolatry, sorcery, enmities, strife, jealousy, outbursts of anger, disputes, dissensions, factions, envying, drunkenness, carousing, and things like these, ... those who practice such things will not inherit the kingdom of God" (Galatians 5:19-21). Conversely, a leader led by the Spirit walks in "Love, joy, peace, patience, kindness, goodness, faithfulness, gentleness, self control" (Galatians 5:22-23). The latter is a picture of clay conforming to the potter's hand. The one who does the deeds of the flesh is a candidate for reshaping. Good leaders love it when followers comply and excel. Be the leader your followers can emulate.

POINTS TO PONDER

When we find ourselves not conforming to the potter's hand, but leaning more toward the pull of the flesh, review this performance check:

> Yield to God's use and desire His total purpose.

> Submit to the Spirit and cultivate inner fruit that honors God.

> Examine how you are contributing to the spiritual shaping of others.

16 /

Practice Makes Perfect

"For the word of God is living and active and sharper than any two edged sword, and piercing as far as the division of soul and spirit, of both joints and marrow, and able to judge the thoughts and intentions of the heart" (Hebrews 4:12, NASB).

When I am suddenly arrested by God's word, it becomes immediately apparent that God is commanding my attention. He is redirecting my swayed focus to sharpen or to compel me to obedience. God sometimes invades my private world because I have lost sight of Him. In all my doing and achieving, I have somehow blundered off the course charted for me by the Christ, my Captain. Secular directives and instructions compel compliance. The Word of the Lord, however, has another effect. It penetrates the heart and compels an obedient response—it is life changing and course changing. His penetrating Word exposes and lays bare all to God (Hebrews 3:13).

So how does the leader practice the presence of God in response to His Word? God gives us every measure of guidance we need: "Your ears will hear a word behind you, 'This is the way, walk in it,' whenever you turn to the right or to the left" (Isaiah 30:21). Ours is to listen, respond and dutifully obey. Some respond to the Word of God with "So what next?" or "Why now?" The sudden squall of God to return to shore is an inconvenience or even a challenge to their plans. Others incorporate His direction and make it an active part of their daily activities. The intentional spiritual leader strives daily to integrate God's directives into his/her thoughts, conversations, and actions (Psalm 119:105). Believing that the greatest impact will come from yielding to the preeminent Word, that leader strives to glorify God through the influence he has in service to others.

The Lord's living and active Word inspires completeness and excellence in each task. It also confirms. Often the Lord says, "Stay the course." Finally, the Word judges and discerns our thoughts. This knowing encourages us to cast every care upon Him (1 Peter 5:7), who alone can handle the full range of human emotion and hurt. We can trust Him with our heart and with our deepest concerns.

POINTS TO PONDER

God's Word changes us! A disciplined regimen of practiced behavior perfects an obedient response to God.

> Pray. Disclose all to the one who knows the intentions of our heart.

> Listen. Be open to confirmation or a change of course (Psalm 119:12).

> Dine wisely. No diet is as effective as daily, full helpings of His Word (Psalm 119:11).

> Share the Lord's guidance. It is effective and beneficial and can produce unimaginable favor in your sphere of influence (Psalm 119:46).

17 /

Reignited Service

"For God has not given to us a spirit of fear, but of power and of love and of a sound mind [discipline]" (2 Timothy 1:7, NKJV).

What is your synonym for "fear?" Is it trepidation, apprehension, alarm or dread? Whatever your definition, that is the side of 2 Timothy 1:7 you need to address. My synonym for "fear" is anxiety. I admit it. I can get anxious about a thing or two. As recently as yesterday I became anxious over an issue. Read 2 Timothy 1:1-14 for a full appreciation of Paul's response to Timothy's fear. Paul acknowledged that Timothy's "sincere faith" (2 Timothy 1:5) was in need of a fresh rekindling (2 Timothy 1:6). God reminded me that dwelling within me is the antidote to fear, which is trust. This reminder led me to an appropriate response to what troubled me. Once I quieted myself, prayed, and then acted, peace returned.

God certainly has not given those who trust Him a spirit of fear. What He has given us, though, is His Holy Spirit, who guides us to apt responses or actions that quell our concerns and calm our anxious hearts. Further, He has given us power, love, and discipline. It is hard to imagine an earthly matter these three cannot surmount. Beware. As with Timothy, fear can cause us to stifle the gift God has given. Do not allow shame (2 Timothy 1:8) or any form of apathy to keep you from living out your call to serve according to His purpose (2 Timothy 1:9). As followers of Christ, as servants, as leaders, we would be well advised to take our own advice. Commit your ways to God and trust Him in your circumstances.

How was your walk with the Lord yesterday? How do you want your walk to be with Him tomorrow? As an act of faith, trust God to reveal the response you need to what concerns you. What other lessons can we draw from Paul's comments to Timothy?

POINTS TO PONDER

> God has entrusted to you a treasured, indwelling gift (2 Timothy 1:14).

> Sometimes we need the help of another to reignite our gift (2 Timothy 1:6).

> Though we may have backed away from what God called us to, He is always willing to reenlist us in service. He wants us to keep our faith on the line (2 Timothy 1:8).

From what fear do you need to be delivered? Rescue is yours for the asking. Trust Him to reignite your gift in faithful service to Him.

18 /

An Actionable Plan

"Then Jesus said to His disciples, 'If anyone wishes to come after Me he must deny himself, and take up his cross and follow Me'" (Matthew 16:24, NKJV).

Who wants to "deny" himself? What does it mean exactly, and how is it done? Look around you and observe. Ours is not a society that particularly thrives on self-denial. I will be the first to say, there is nothing wrong with having. The problem comes when possessions have us and when our minds are not on God's interests but on man's (Matthew 16:23-27). It is not natural to give up our self-interest or to sacrifice for others. The thought of doing without is not an ingredient the typical leader prefers. We do not like having fewer resources than the mission requires. However, we must ask ourselves what might be facilitated through self-denial and in making Christ our all (Colossians 3:11). Denial of self might translate to, "But whoever loses his life for My sake will find it" (Matthew 16:25b). Joy in service then becomes the by product of giving oneself unreservedly to God's interests.

Self-denial leads to the possibility of flourishing, both professionally and spiritually. It might lead one to integrate faith with one's profession. Where do the two intersect? One might ask if there is anything "actionable" that shows one how to take up his cross or that projects spiritual integrity into the workplace. Some professions require an oath to demonstrate commitment to the profession. The Christian and Christian leader must also determine the extent of his or her faith commitment in service.

One might think that through self-denial one forfeits what is due him. The opposite is true. Through such renunciation, we gain and what is given up is repaid (Matthew 16:27). God knows what we give up in service to Him. The fact that He will "repay" represents His recognition and appreciation. While our flesh does not like the idea of giving up or accepting less, it benefits us to do so. In the words of Jim Elliot, "He is no fool who gives what he cannot keep to gain what he cannot lose." The leader whose commander is the Lord knows who controls his destiny (Matthew 16:25a). The tug of fleshly desires is weakened when I take my mind off my own interests and focus on God's interests. When I do that, I am, in effect, denying myself.

POINTS TO PONDER

> Are justice, kindness, and humble service the tenor of your leadership? (Micah 6:8).

> Are you genuinely concerned for the welfare of others? (Philippians 2:20).

> As you consider workplace or home productivity, are you willing to be ruled by godly wisdom even if it runs counter to your "get-it-done-now" approach? (Colossians 4:5-6).

Monthly Reflection

Monthly Reflection

It's time for a quick evaluation. Use this section to help gauge your habit of integrating faith and profession, and to help get you into the habit of keeping a written record of those times when the Holy Spirit speaks to you. Use the questions below for monthly reflection and to aid a spiritual approach to challenges confronting your application of faith and leadership. The questions are intended for the purpose of self-reflection and contemplation—not guilt and self-loathing.

1. Among your daily requirements, were you able to achieve aside time with God through personal reading of Scripture and prayer?

☐ Yes
☐ No

2. Recall one or two of the most significant leadership challenges you encountered over the past 30 days. What was your response to the challenge(s) and what effect, if any, did your spiritual development priority have on how you addressed the situation?

_____
_____
_____
_____
_____
_____
_____
_____
_____
_____
_____
_____

3. Reflecting over the past 30 days, name one or two ways you met balance between work and family requirements.

_____
_____
_____
_____
_____
_____
_____
_____
_____
_____
_____
_____

4. Have you recently observed an event that you would count as answered prayer?

☐ Yes (explain) _____
_____

☐ No

5. Did you enlist the aid of a prayer partner over the last 30 days?

☐ Yes
☐ No

19 /

Faith Rhythm

"But without faith it is impossible to please Him, for he who comes to God must believe that He is, and that He is a rewarder of those who diligently seek Him" (Hebrews 11:6, NKJV).

Faith expresses not only belief in God's redemptive act, but also active acceptance of the Lord's palpable presence in our lives. God is for us and thus permeates our thoughts, prayers, and actions. Confidence in God's redemptive act must be without degree, yet our behavior as those who believe in the God of the Holy Scriptures is marked with imperfection. Those listed in Hebrews "faith hall of fame" were faithful, but they were also fallible human beings who committed faithless acts. Faith marks itself in acts of belief in the character of God and in His faithfulness to us through Himself.

The better we understand God's character, the better we will demonstrate belief. As a young 21-year-old, I checked myself into the hospital for significant surgery that would medically qualify me for an Air Force commission. With no health insurance and less than five dollars to my name, I took action consistent with my belief that God would take care of the hospital bill. I did not know how He would do this, but I had no doubt that He would provide. The day following my surgery, two men walked into my hospital room. They said, "We want to pay your hospital bill." I was blown away! These people did not know me nor I them, and I don't know how they found me or how they knew of my need. I signed a form and that was the end of it. I never even received a bill. "Faithful is He who calls you, and He also will bring it to pass" (1 Thessalonians 5:24, NASB). I expected God would work something out for my medical expenses, and He did. He did it right away. That said, how does one reconcile results that go contrary to what one prays?

Jesus' disciples witnessed the immediate demise of a fig tree (Matthew

21:19). Jesus responded, "If you have faith and do not doubt, you will not only do what was done to the fig tree, but even if you say to this mountain, be taken up and cast into the sea, it will happen." This was not the first time Jesus called out the disciples' faith. However, Jesus' statement, "If you have faith and do not doubt," should lead those who call themselves followers of Christ to check their faith or belief rhythm.

Do you maintain a barometer of your expressed faith? Jesus said, "All things you ask in prayer, believing, you will receive" (Matthew 21:22). This is not "name it and claim it." This is not, "I know what is best, so hand it over, God." This is "nevertheless, not my will but thine be done." If we falter in unbelief when our prayers seem to go unanswered, let us not fail to recognize who is in the boat with us. "Why are you afraid, you men of little faith? Then He got up and rebuked the winds and the sea, and it became perfectly calm" (Matthew 8:26). Our belief should be that God will maintain the integrity of His character and that He will do good for us in the final analysis. Yes, I hear it. The words of the father whose boy was tormented by a spirit echo in my heart: "I do believe; help my unbelief" (Mark 9:24). How do we hit a faith rhythm that repeatedly expresses belief without doubt, belief that what we ask will be done according to His will?

Faith, like any muscle, requires exercise. Faith enlarges our leadership effectiveness, enables us to achieve the mission, and makes us more capable of serving others. Those who follow your lead will note your faith in action and prayerfully glorify God.

POINTS TO PONDER

> Pray and Rejoice. Let prayer and thanksgiving be our ready response (1 Thessalonians 5:16-18).

> Believe. Trust and have confidence in knowing that God always acts according to His will (Thessalonians 5:24).

> Genuine faith is active. Commit your ways to God, and trust his leading (1 Thessalonians 5:21 and Psalm 37:5, 7)

20 /
Big-Picture Perspective

"And when His disciples James and John saw this, they said, 'Lord, do You want us to command fire to come down from heaven and consume them, just as Elijah did?'" (Luke 9:54, NKJV).

There are few things in life I know for certain. I can be wrong; I am subject to make mistakes. I cannot help but wonder about James and John when they cited Elijah's act of calling down fire from heaven to destroy the messengers from Samaria (2 Kings 1:10, 12). Apparently, they saw some parallels between the Old Testament Samaritan king Ahaziah's response to the man of God (Elijah) and the Samaritans who did not welcome Jesus at His arrival (Luke 9:52). James and John perhaps succumbed to a mistaken understanding of Jesus' purpose.

Sometimes, we respond from ignorance either through lack of compassion or failure to grasp the big picture. James and John's compassionless desire to call fire down from heaven on a people, who would later welcome Jesus and the gospel into their borders (John 4:39-41), demonstrates not only a lack of compassion, but also insensitivity to Jesus' bigger purpose. Jesus' response to James and John's desire to rain down death and destruction gives us the Master's leadership attitude, one which we should emulate in response to personal rejection.

Servant leaders who seek to minister to all people groups must do so with a spirit of compassion (Luke 9:55b, NASB). The compassionate Christian leader would do well to strive to express the heart of Christ. Controlled and sparingly used, anger or aggression might be an appropriate response to quell selfish, sinful acts. However, the decision to turn from hot emotions as a response to rejection and insensitivity and to "shake the dust off your feet" (Luke 9:5), can lead one to turn to Christ for His big picture perspective. This demonstrates the better part of spiritual valor.

Jesus said He "did not come to destroy lives but to save them" (Luke 9:56, NASB). If one's tendency is to write people off when there is disagreement, might this have the same effect as "commanding fire" or wishing another dead, spiritually dead that is. The gospel message is for all people and the servant leader does not withhold the message at the first sign of personal rejection.

POINTS TO PONDER

Consider this Spirit directed response to tough circumstances, resistance, or rejection:

> Pray. Ask God for His perspective and for a compassionate spirit when dealing with difficult people. Desire to know the heart of Christ when emotions would evoke an angry, fleshly response.

> Practice. Exercise patience with others, especially those who seem insensitive or ignorant to spiritual matters. Patience manifests compassion and replaces anger and aggression with gentleness and sincere concern.

> Picture. Focus on the big picture. Appreciate the fact that God has a far larger perspective and plan than we sometimes comprehend. Strive to be in sync with God. It is not His desire that any should perish.

21 /

Commander's Intent

God said to Moses, "I AM WHO I AM"; and He said, "Thus you shall say to the sons of Israel, 'I AM has sent me to you'" (Exodus 3:14, NASB).

Ever had the feeling of being inadequate for a task, but deep down inside you knew you had to take it on? The situation or event was yours to win or lose, but your internalized anxiety hindered your ability to believe that things would end well. That lack of faith is not the Commander's desire for us. Rather, His intent is that we stretch ourselves to demonstrate bold and courageous faith. The faith required to act on the seemingly unfeasible plans of God may take us well outside our comfort zones. It may well force a confession or a denial of God's sufficiency, of His simply being enough. Moses had a similar dilemma.

Moses made many excuses. He could visualize no plan that resulted in successfully bringing God's people out of Egypt. Moses might have thought: Lord, what you're asking me to do is impossible. He asked, "Who am I?" (Exodus 3:11). God did not ask Moses if he wanted to go to Pharaoh. He told him, I am sending you (Exodus 3:10). In so doing, He extended to Moses the assurance that he (Moses) was indeed sufficient for the task because God himself would be present: "I will be with you" (Exodus 3:12). Later in Exodus 33:15, Moses declares, "If your presence will not go (with us), do not carry us up from this place." Though Moses' response is still tenuous, he is coming to understand the power that accompanies His presence. Distress and discouragement—the unwelcomed duo—are banned from His presence. Anxiety is checked at the door, and faithlessness becomes courageous faith in action.

God will do no less for the committed servant leader than He would do for Moses. He will act to uproot discouragement and, often, remove obstacles (Exodus 3:20). He will give favor in the face of the unreasonable, and will prevail over disagreeable circumstances (Exodus 3:21). We must come to see the right and necessary action as His idea, His plan, and His intention. We must come to terms with the action of an infallible God choosing fallible man to execute His great plans (Exodus 3:22).

When faced with matters that seem insurmountable, revisit the full text of God's mission for Moses (Exodus 3:10-22), move ahead in faith, and walk confidently in the assurance of God's presence in demanding circumstances. Courageously strive to fulfill His intent.

POINTS TO PONDER

> God gives insight, creativity, and wisdom to meet all tasks He asks of us. Trust His leadership (Exodus 3:20; Isaiah 30:21).

> When done according to His plan, no necessary action is unfeasible. Express confidence in God's promised presence and faithfulness (Exodus 3:12).

> Rely on God's provision. Feasibility studies are said to be the doorway to action. Make your stand here: God is trustworthy and true.

22 /

Lasting Influence

"Then the LORD said to Noah, 'Enter the ark, you and all your household, for you alone I have seen to be righteous before Me in this time'" (Genesis 7:1, NASB).

In the midst of man's evil and God's displeasure with him, Noah found favor "in the eyes of God" (Genesis 6:8). When all around you are caught up in misbehavior, unethical practices and wickedness, how should you respond? Noah's example gives us a significant testimony of godly behavior and influence in the home that we can also adopt as leaders in the workplace. Noah refused to compromise amidst mass self-indulgence and lawlessness (Genesis 6:5-6). Father to three sons—Shem, Ham, and Japheth—Noah erected a lasting, godly influence for them and for us. Noah behaved honorably and did not allow the evil of his day to shape him. "Noah was a righteous man, blameless in his time; Noah walked with God" (Genesis 6:9). He cultivated right thinking and keen discernment, a safeguard for the godly in an ungodly culture.

When we have our eyes set on godly living, the lust of the flesh has no attraction. We will dare to do bold things for God, and we will influence others. Noah was 600 years old when he, his wife, his sons, and their wives boarded the ark. For roughly 100 years while the ark was under construction, Noah's convincing example was so credible that his sons followed their father's lead throughout the project. And what of the centuries before construction started? The Lord's commendation is "You alone I have seen to be righteous before me in this time" (Genesis 7:1). Cynics will say: No one else listened to Noah. Why is he such a noteworthy person? As a father and leader, the more I think of Noah's influence in his sons' lives, the more it blows me away. He reared three boys without rebellion in those pre-Flood days!

What has God commissioned you to do? In your vocation or avocation, are you aware of the influence that your obedience is positioning you to wield? In your home, church, community, and work, steady obedience to God's always perfect, sometimes counter intuitive directions for living is still the way to distinguish yourself for God in your time. Positive influence on others requires full obedience (Genesis 7:5). I am impressed that Noah's influence over his sons was greater than the negative influences around them. Noah honored God, and his sons followed suit.

POINTS TO PONDER

We can learn much about influencing others from God's commendation of Noah.

> Be intentional about making a lasting, positive influence in the life of another.

> Be aware that influence is often a function of others watching our non polished or non published actions.

> Obediently perform what God has given you to do and keep at it.

Monthly Reflection

Monthly Reflection

It's time for a quick evaluation. Use this section to help gauge your habit of integrating faith and profession, and to help get you into the habit of keeping a written record of those times when the Holy Spirit speaks to you. Use the questions below for monthly reflection and to aid a spiritual approach to challenges confronting your application of faith and leadership. The questions are intended for the purpose of self-reflection and contemplation—not guilt and self-loathing.

1. Among your daily requirements, were you able to achieve aside time with God through personal reading of Scripture and prayer?

☐ Yes
☐ No

2. Recall one or two of the most significant leadership challenges you encountered over the past 30 days. What was your response to the challenge(s) and what effect, if any, did your spiritual development priority have on how you addressed the situation?

_____
_____
_____
_____
_____
_____
_____
_____
_____
_____
_____
_____
_____

3. Reflecting over the past 30 days, name one or two ways you met balance between work and family requirements.

_____
_____
_____
_____
_____
_____
_____
_____
_____
_____
_____
_____

4. Have you recently observed an event that you would count as answered prayer?

☐ Yes (explain) _____
_____

☐ No

5. Did you enlist the aid of a prayer partner over the last 30 days?

☐ Yes
☐ No

23 /
What Say Ye?

"When Jesus saw the crowds, He went up on the mountain; and after He sat down, His disciples came to Him. He opened His mouth and began to teach them saying…" (Matthew 5:1-2, NASB).

How do you behave in a crowd? How do you know what to do and what not to do? Does your Christ like behavior identify you as different, and do others find you approachable? Jesus' demeanor generally drew others to Him. He was not prickly, rude, arrogant, or stingy with His wisdom. On the hillside where He delivered the beatitudes, Jesus in the presence of many and in the company of His disciples freely shared wisdom for living.

For many who lead and influence others, the right words may not always seem self-evident. One may be tempted to play it safe by delivering some writer's scripted lines or by taking the path of least resistance in the arenas of work or relationships. When it is not clear exactly what to say, we can safely rely on God's Spirit for guidance. The presence of the Holy Spirit will aid in knowing how and what to speak (Isaiah 30:21). Jesus sat on a hillside and out came words for living, words relevant to each and every one who listened. Being fully God, Jesus could be expected to know what to speak to every man, but what about us mortals? As we set Christ apart in our hearts (1 Peter 3:15) and make studying God's word a priority, we too can know how to answer every man, whether in the board room, at a lunch table, in the workplace or on the golf course.

Jesus also encountered individuals, including the solitary woman at the well (John 4:6-26). Likewise, many of our encounters occur one on one and are no less significant than large group interactions. They may, in fact, be more significant or impactful. The issue often boils down to speaking when the Spirit prompts! Knowing how to respond actually starts before the encounter. Time spent in reading, studying, meditating, and memorizing Scripture will extensively aid how the Spirit directs conversation.

When we do not fully grasp all the parameters of the here and now, the Holy Spirit does and will give understanding at the right time. The disciples did not fully grasp all of Jesus' teachings while in His presence. They grew in depth of understanding as they continued in the Scriptures (Peter and John in Acts 4:13 and Stephen in Acts 6:10) and in the Spirit.

How about you? Are you discerning God's voice when you find yourself speaking to many, a few, or one on one? Just as Jesus spent much time in prayer and solitude with God, the basis of our responses may be proportional to the time we spend with God in study of the Scriptures.

POINTS TO PONDER

The Holy Spirit gives conversation discernment as we…

\> Spend time with God in study (2 Timothy 2:15).

\> Trust the Spirit for the response (Matthew 10:19-20).

\> Listen for His voice (Isaiah 30:21).

24 /

Are You Leading?

"Then Jesus said to him, 'Put your sword back into its place; for all those who take up the sword shall perish by the sword. Or do you think that I cannot appeal to My Father, and He will at once put at My disposal more than twelve legions of angels? How then will the Scriptures be fulfilled, which say that it must happen this way?'" (Matthew 26:52-54, NASB).

Jesus wielded His influence—not his power—to accomplish the prophecies concerning Him. Man's natural inclination is to think: He who carries the biggest stick wins. That wasn't the case when Judas, who betrayed Jesus, arrived with the arresting party who would ultimately be responsible for Jesus' crucifixion. Instead of condoning Peter's (John 18:10-11) protective gesture of striking the high priest's servant, Jesus healed the injury Peter inflicted and told him to put away his weapon.

Jesus could have commanded a greater force than Peter's dagger. He could have responded to the arresting entourage with a show of His mighty power or through a simple appeal to his Father who would have put thousands of angels at the ready for Jesus' use as He pleased. Instead He identified Himself as the one they sought (John 18:5). A good leader becomes self evident by his actions. That is, one leads best when one's actions reflect decisions arrived at through calm, calculated, inspired thought rather than reckless displays of power. Jesus did that. He told Peter to put away his sword. His command to Peter reveals that leaders who use overwhelming displays of power are not always effective at accomplishing the mission.

Jesus' mission was to ensure the prophecies concerning Him would be fulfilled. His leadership style was that of influence and not the use of "shock and awe." Faith and leadership are therefore more appropriately modeled through keeping sight of how to achieve God's purposes in and out of the workplace through godly influence, using softer tones, quieter approaches and direct resolve to see the mission through. Simply acting or reacting is not necessarily an effective leadership quality. Leading entails helping people see the bigger picture when "it must happen this way."

POINTS TO PONDER

Consider the following questions as a possible test of how effectively you are integrating your faith and leadership through influence in your workplace or place of service.

> How do you respond to inaccurate or injurious comments? Do you fire back with insults, or are you exercising servant-leader restraint? (1 Peter 2:23).

> How effectively do you take the spiritual high road when resolving conflicts? (James 1:20 and Proverbs 15:1).

> When project goals are seemingly being thwarted, do you entertain the idea that God can also work through this opposition? (Romans 8:28 and Acts 8:1).

25 /

Your Every Need

"And my God will supply every need of yours according to his riches in glory in Christ Jesus" (Philippians 4:19, ESV).

"He has been mighty good to me!" "God is good, all the time. All the time; God is good." I have heard these phrases expressed, somewhat emotionally, at church testimony meetings and other places. These expressions are true and, most often, heartfelt.

Paul's statement in Philippians 4:19 seems a culmination of his gratefulness for the kindness shown him by the believers mentioned in Philippians 4:10-19. Additionally, Paul's joyful comments give testimony of God's faithfulness to meet his needs. Though Paul expressed heartfelt thanks for the gift, at the same time, he seems to stand the act of giving on it head: It is not that those who give satisfy needs, but it is God who uses generous givers to meet needs (Philippians 4:13).

Those who are generous toward God will find that He is generous toward them and will supply their every need in Christ Jesus. Expressed another way, giving is receiving. I am inspired by Paul's obvious absence of anxiety as to whether God would give him what he needed. Paul was not concerned for material gifts; his greatest concern was the potential spiritual harvest to be reaped through their generosity (Philippians 4:17). Yet, Paul makes a more far reaching statement: If you had any concerns about parting with your gifts, don't. Instead, know as I know that, "God will supply every need of yours." His comments clearly extended beyond concern for material needs.

What leader is not concerned with maximizing his/her time use or hasn't felt the insufficiency of time in a day to meet all requirements? And what about the challenge of needing fresh insight and perspective in confronting problems? "God will supply every need of yours" whether it is a financial concern, effective time management, or dealing with disgruntled people. Jesus is the resource for all our needs. As faithful followers, ours is to approach Him confidently for grace and help (Hebrews 4:16).

POINTS TO PONDER

> In what areas of work, home, or community service do you especially need help?

> How are you trusting God to meet all your needs, i.e., time management, wisdom, and resources?

> How might those nearest you describe or affirm your unwavering belief that God will supply your every need?

26 /

Loyalty

"As they were reclining at the table and eating, Jesus said, 'Truly I say to you that one of you will betray Me—one who is eating with Me'" (Mark 14:18, ESV).

Why do you think Jesus raised the subject of his betrayal? Why did He tell the disciples someone would betray Him? Perhaps He simply needed to tell someone who cared. Jesus told his disciples. He said it not once but, according to Mark, approached the matter five times (Mark 14:18, 27, 30, 34, and 36). The fifth time He poured His heart out to His Father (Mark 14:36). At Jesus' comment, the disciples questioned their loyalty.

To be loyal is to show allegiance and to demonstrate constant support. This fidelity defines the leader/follower relationship. Disloyalty hurts. At the Passover meal the disciples had the opportunity to examine their own constancy to Christ. As followers of Christ, it is prudent to examine our trustworthiness and to monitor that which could allure, even lull us into thoughtless words and deeds. Jesus' loyalty was without question. He said, "…I will never leave you nor forsake you" (Hebrews 13:5b).

Loyalty is demonstrated in the workplace for many noble reasons: belief in the cause or product or allegiance to the institution. The follower of Christ must understand his or her own motives for following and serving. Rightly motivated, believers respond to God's demonstrated love for us (Romans 5:8). Did you notice that the one who betrayed Him reclined at the table and was eating with Him? Judas was a recipient of fellowship, inclusion, identity, and belonging without comprehending that loyalty is a two-way street. Jesus paid the price of his commitment to us on the cross. Are we willing to pay the price of loyalty to Him? More aptly, why am I willing to pay the price of constancy to Christ?

POINTS TO PONDER

> When you are tested, tempted, worn out, and perhaps overcommitted, how might your loyalty to Christ waver? (Mark 14:37-38).

> "There is no fear in love; but perfect love casts out fear, because fear involves punishment, and the one who fears is not perfected in love" (1 John 4:18, NASB). How is your love relationship with Jesus?

> What motivates your loyalty to Christ—the love relationship, the reward, or both?

27 /

What Do You Want From Me?

"You are those who have stood by Me in My trials" (Luke 22:28, NASB).

How well are you sensing what God desires of you? A reading of Luke 22:27-32 might lead you to respond that constancy is what the Lord wants of you. It is normal to tire of struggles. God knows we will be tried, but in our trials He yearns for us to keep at it and not give up. Evil forces are always gunning to take down a good team (Luke 22:31). Regardless of how impervious one might think he is, the occasion to fall exists (1 Corinthians 10:12). Christ commended the disciples for standing with Him in his trials. What a critical teaching point. This perseverance in the face of challenge would be required of them individually and as a team.

The disciples had been with Jesus for three years, and little did they know they would be the leaders of the world's Christianity movement. Not surprisingly, the responsibility to teach and train others most often falls to the one who has experienced the event. In our society a qualifying requirement of a leader is experience. Jesus flatly said to His disciples: You've been there, you have seen what I have been through, you have heard my explanations, and you saw me in my trials—you "have stood by Me." In no uncertain terms, Jesus told the disciples they would be leaders who would sit in judgment in His kingdom (Luke 22:30).

This kind of leadership and authority would come at a cost. For Peter and for many of us that cost would be testing, even the possibility of failure (Luke 22:32). Our response to trials will either strengthen or arrest us. The elect must not turn back but continue to serve and edify others. Keep at it; don't give up. Be counted among those who "stood by Me in my trials."

POINTS TO PONDER

> Will it be said that you "stood by" Him against the popular culture, in the midst of

calls to compromise, and despite your natural intuition or desires?

> How is your faith when the going gets tough? Know that the trial of your faith is to the praise, honor, and glory of Jesus Christ (1 Peter 1:7).

> Ask yourself: Am I still working at what I thought the Lord called me to or have I quietly moved on to other interests?

What does Jesus want from you? That your faith not fail, that you keep turning to Him, and finally, that you lead by encouraging and strengthening others who face similar circumstances. Be encouraged, Jesus stands by you.

Monthly Reflection

Monthly Reflection

It's time for a quick evaluation. Use this section to help gauge your habit of integrating faith and profession, and to help get you into the habit of keeping a written record of those times when the Holy Spirit speaks to you. Use the questions below for monthly reflection and to aid a spiritual approach to challenges confronting your application of faith and leadership. The questions are intended for the purpose of self-reflection and contemplation—not guilt and self-loathing.

1. Among your daily requirements, were you able to achieve aside time with God through personal reading of Scripture and prayer?

☐ Yes
☐ No

2. Recall one or two of the most significant leadership challenges you encountered over the past 30 days. What was your response to the challenge(s) and what effect, if any, did your spiritual development priority have on how you addressed the situation?

_____
_____
_____
_____
_____
_____
_____
_____
_____
_____
_____
_____

3. Reflecting over the past 30 days, name one or two ways you met balance between work and family requirements.

_____
_____
_____
_____
_____
_____
_____
_____
_____
_____

4. Have you recently observed an event that you would count as answered prayer?

☐ Yes (explain) _____
_____

☐ No

5. Did you enlist the aid of a prayer partner over the last 30 days?

☐ Yes
☐ No

28 /

Let Us Go

"On that day, when evening came, He said to them, 'Let us go over to the other side'" (Mark 4:35, NASB).

Jesus and the disciples set out on what seemed to have been a normal day. The weather must have been agreeable for a boat ride across the lake, when suddenly, while Jesus was "in the stern asleep on the cushion," (Mark 4:38) they found themselves in the midst of a storm. Had the experienced fishermen turned disciples known a storm was coming, surely they would have opted out of the boat ride to cross the lake.

I once had a boss whose common saying was: Don't associate yourself with a disaster. Following that kind of leadership advice, the experienced fishermen would perhaps have never gotten in the boat. However, Jesus was not caught off guard by the storm and undoubtedly designed the lesson that would follow.

This experience would teach the disciples and serve to re emphasize to us that we need not fear when the unexpected arises. God controls the wind and the rain (Jonah 1:4-5). Though the disciples were fearful and helpless, they knew to whom to turn in the midst of sudden fear and apparent disaster (Mark 4:38). Jesus wants us to have faith, trusting that He is with us. Absent His physical presence, we can still rest in Christ's full knowledge of each prevailing circumstance (Mark 6:48). Jesus walked across the water and joined them in the midst of their trial and reassured them.

Going "over to the other side" is a poignant metaphor for living by faith. Jesus asked His disciples, "Why are you afraid? Do you still have no faith?" (Mark 4:40). He Himself had said, "Let us go to the other side." Reasonably, He had every intention of arriving fully intact at the destination to which He had said, "Let us go." God cannot doubt Himself and those who travel with Him are asked not to doubt, as well. Leaders appreciate it when followers have confidence in their word. Jesus expects no less of His followers. Choose a faith walk that relies on Christ's reliability.

POINTS TO PONDER

> Do not deny in a crisis what you know to be true about God's reliability (Romans 14:22).

> God's silence should not be misconstrued as unconcern (Hebrews 13:5b-6a).

> When decisions and actions prove difficult and fear invades, do not falter in the face of the untenable. Rather, approach each trial with immovable faith (Philippians 1:6).

29 /

A Soldier's Memorial

"And fixing his gaze on him and being much alarmed, he said, 'What is it, Lord?' And he said to him, 'Your prayers and alms have ascended as a memorial before God'" (Acts 10:4, NASB).

What do you want to be remembered for? On Memorial Day we remember fallen veterans and others who were dear to us. Memorial Day is a time for reflecting and honoring heroic actions of many who lived out their convictions and a day to demonstrate that their sacrifices were not in vain.

The Scriptures give various accounts of events worthy of memorialization down through the ages. The "good deed" of the woman who anointed Jesus "beforehand for the burial" (Mark 14:8) is one such account. Jesus stated her act would subsequently be "spoken of in memory of her" (Mark 14:9). Death, however, need not be the event that delivers lasting memorials. Cornelius, a centurion, a leader of leaders, and a soldier is memorialized in Scripture for his consistent prayers and good deeds. An angel spoke to Cornelius and said, "Your prayers and alms have ascended as a memorial before God." The Spirit of God used Cornelius to intervene in the life of Peter the Apostle and to deliver the gospel to the Gentiles (Acts 10:34-48). Cornelius' devout life and reverence for God influenced his entire household and left an enduring spiritual legacy for generations.

Conscientious leaders strive to establish a positive legacy, and when it is time to move on, they usually pass the function or office on in better condition than they received it. Cornelius was obviously a faithful soldier. He gave time and attention to the spiritual dimension of his life, and God recognized his spiritual acts of prayer and generosity. Similarly, the woman who anointed Jesus' head did so in spite of criticism. With determined conviction, she offered this unselfish act of service.

Cornelius did not set out to be remembered. He had the responsibility of leading soldiers and his family. His devotion to God was neither a hindrance nor an afterthought. It was his habit to beseech God on behalf of others and to do what was in his power to assist. A focused leader and faithful believer, Cornelius seamlessly integrated his faith with his profession and availed himself for God's use. This "devout man" (Acts 10:2) pleased the Lord and received His commendation. What about you? How are you consistently availing yourself for Christ's service?

POINTS TO PONDER

> How would you like to be remembered by God and by others? What matters most to you, man's impression or God's?

> Are you responsive to the legitimate needs of others when approached for help (non monetary matters)? How are you using your time, talent and treasures for Kingdom building? No faithful act is insignificant.

> How are you actively living out your faith? Do you encourage others to do likewise?

30 /

Strengthen Yourself

"Then the prophet came near to the king of Israel and said to him, 'Go strengthen yourself and observe and see what you have to do; for at the turn of the year the king of Aram will come up against you'" (1 Kings 20:22, NASB).

There is much to be said for taking advantage of the right time to rest and gain perspective in anticipation of what might lie ahead. With a certainty, we can be assured troubles will come, sooner or later. As seasons change, so do the realities of daily living. A consideration of how the Lord provided in the past provides fuel to go the distance when the unexpected occurs.

King Ahab's wars with the Aramean's King Ben-hadad are described in 1 Kings 20. Israel's small army was not allied with other nations as was the Aramean army. In fact, King Ben-hadad had pushed Israel around, requiring Israel's silver, gold, women and children (1 Kings 20:3). Not until the Lord put an end to Israel's acquiescence did Ahab stand up to Ben-hadad (1 Kings 20:13-14). By a surprise attack, Ben-haded found himself in retreat (1 Kings 20:20) with plans to re attack Israel in the spring (1 Kings 20:22).

Intimidation, threats, and the unknown have a way of manufacturing fear and anxiety. However, God's wisdom is available to us. God's prophet gave Ahab answers, the way ahead, and confidence. Today—God's Word and His abiding presence (Psalm 3:1-5) steady us when we are facing great and small obstacles. As with Ahab, the very things that are not obvious to us, the Lord uses as His tool to deliver us (1 Kings 20:14).

At the corner of triumph is not the place to pull back and declare, "game over, problem solved." It is time to do as the prophet told King Ahab: "strengthen yourself," recoup, and be ready for what lies ahead. Rest in the Lord and reflect on His presence—even when His presence may seem less apparent. Know that conditions will change, but the Lord's presence never does. The unexpected need not derail us as we lean on Him, for it is God who guides and helps. The one whose confidence is in the Lord has no weakness a foe can take advantage of (1 Kings 20:28-30). May the Lord be our guide in all circumstances and may He daily strengthen us to be suited for whatever comes our way.

POINTS TO PONDER

> How are you resting in God? Is He your very present help in times of trouble? (Psalm 46:1).

> What do you need to do to be ready for unexpected troubles? (1 Peter 5:8).

> Have you resolved not to allow evil to rule or dictate your behavior? Are you likely to retaliate with an eye for an eye, or do grace and compassion dictate your reaction to evil? (Psalm 25:2).

31 /

Condition of Service

"I thank Christ Jesus our Lord, who has strengthened me, because He considered me faithful, putting me into service" (1 Timothy 1:12, NASB).

Do you have the reputation of being the "go to guy?" Weighty responsibility and promise can accompany this reputation. What qualified you for such acclaim? What achievement or characteristic elevates someone over another? If you have started formulating a mental checklist of "go to guy" virtues, stop right here and consider the qualifications Paul designates believers should strive for as they advance the kingdom of God: Love from a pure heart, a good conscience, and sincere faith (1 Timothy 1:5).
One complication with being the reputed point man can be our temptation to take credit for what God enables us to do. In other words, our good reputation could serve as a thief of the Lord's glory. How God has gifted us as administrators, leaders, or teachers are gifts that can be mishandled in that we use them to divert exaltation from the Gifter.

Faithfulness to Christ Jesus is the desired end state. What Christ has entrusted to us, He wants us to offer back to Him in faithful service to others. In the Old Testament, the Lord gifted certain people with skills and technical knowledge to build artifacts for the temple. God led them to construct things for His own glory, not for the builders' glory. In that sense, God's calling us into service can be a fragile honor, something to be handled with great care. It has been said, "a little knowledge can puff one up." Paul observed that some strayed and ended in fruitlessness (1 Timothy 1:6). The goal and privilege of believers is to serve Christ again, and again, and again. The applause we want to hear comes from the Lord saying, "Well done good and faithful servant." I am keeping you in service.

It is a privilege to be called into service and given skills by Him to shape programs that will draw people to Him. Our goal is not to amass a personal reputation as the qualified "go to person," but rather to point others to Him for the glory He is due. As God calls us into service, He does not call us because of our unique skill set or qualifications; rather, He deems us faithful and trustworthy as a condition for service.

POINTS TO PONDER

> Are your acts of service done with a pure heart, a good conscience, and sincere faith? (Psalm 119:2).

> Having performed a job "well done," would your closest associates, if asked, cite your skills or both your skills and faith in God for the work you do? (1 Timothy 1:17).

Monthly Reflection

Monthly Reflection

It's time for a quick evaluation. Use this section to help gauge your habit of integrating faith and profession, and to help get you into the habit of keeping a written record of those times when the Holy Spirit speaks to you. Use the questions below for monthly reflection and to aid a spiritual approach to challenges confronting your application of faith and leadership. The questions are intended for the purpose of self-reflection and contemplation—not guilt and self-loathing.

1. Among your daily requirements, were you able to achieve aside time with God through personal reading of Scripture and prayer?

☐ Yes
☐ No

2. Recall one or two of the most significant leadership challenges you encountered over the past 30 days. What was your response to the challenge(s) and what effect, if any, did your spiritual development priority have on how you addressed the situation?

_____
_____
_____
_____
_____
_____
_____
_____
_____
_____
_____
_____

3. Reflecting over the past 30 days, name one or two ways you met balance between work and family requirements.

4. Have you recently observed an event that you would count as answered prayer?

☐ Yes (explain)

☐ No

5. Did you enlist the aid of a prayer partner over the last 30 days?

☐ Yes
☐ No

32 /

Restoration

"He will sit as a smelter and purifier of silver, and He will purify the sons of Levi and refine them like gold and silver, so that they may present to the LORD offerings in righteousness" (Malachi 3:3, NASB).

Will I be an agent of restoration? Restoration has to do with being allowed to get back on the right path. It occurs when one has erred, paid the price and repented of the error. Restoration allows one to prove that true, permanent, positive change has occurred.

Often servant leaders have the opportunity to practice being an agent of restoration. What causes us to second-guess whether a person deserves a second try? Perhaps it has to do with not wanting to give counterparts the impression of weakness, of questionable judgment or of being a soft touch.

Should desire to keep up good impressions with peers and counterparts replace God's restorative act? In the sight of the Lord, restoration might be a multiple part process. Psalm 23:3 says, "He restores my soul; He guides me in the paths of righteousness for His name sake." God restores and renders fit for service the repentant one who confesses sin (1 John 1:9). In Malachi 3, God announced the sending of a messenger who would purify the priests, making what was "not fit for service, fit for service." The act of purification restores a person or thing to the original value.

Whether I accept the prerogative of being an agent of restoration or not, it will not nullify the cleansing power and restoration God grants through confession and repentance. Cleansing and restoration has everything to do with the integrity of who God is. As God completes His refining process, we must be mindful that if we want God to forgive us, we must be willing to forgive and help restore others.

POINTS TO PONDER

> Would you say you are an agent of restoration in word or deed? Forgiveness is a noble act that helps facilitate restoration (2 Corinthians 2:7).

> What role can our words play in the restorative process? (Colossians 4:6).

> In real terms, think of the purifying cycle as spiritual breathing. When we confess our sins, we exhale. We inhale by receiving God's forgiveness (1 John 1:9).

33 /

Himself for Me

"I have been crucified with Christ; and it is no longer I who live, but Christ lives in me; and the life which I now live in the flesh I live by faith in the Son of God, who loved me and gave Himself up for me" (Galatians 2:20, NASB).

What does total commitment look like or mean to the one who has given full allegiance to God? It means much, however shifting resolve is not part of the description. Paul uttered this exceptional declaration and made it clear that obedience to Christ could reflect disloyalty to some of the practices of man, especially if they are at odds with what God is asking us to do. Paul's commitment to Christ meant he would not fluctuate between possibilities, nor flicker when faced with adversity; he would not grow weary and lose heart in the face of opposition (Hebrews 12:3). The committed, dutiful follower does not surrender when he draws fire for his faith. Frankly, Paul is expressing gratitude and trust in the One who first demonstrated His commitment for him. Christ's resolve and love are exhibited in Jesus giving "Himself up for me."

A desire to trade places with a sick loved one shows a compelling display of total commitment. However, loyalty to others should pale in comparison to what we offer the One who gave Himself up for us.

"I have been crucified with Christ." In his statement Paul recognizes that his sinful nature had been set aside or done away with (Romans 6:6). He embraced the fact that sin had lost its grip on him. He was a changed man. The soldier lives by the written and spoken orders of his superiors. Paul affirms, "The life I now live… I live by faith in the Son of God." In loyalty, Paul looked to Christ for courage to live by faith and to trust Him with life's difficulties.

In a practical sense, Paul yielded to Jesus' "all in" commitment and gave up attempts to be to people what God never intended him to be. He surrendered himself to Christ's love and determined to lead a life of faith. Christ was and is "all in." What about you? In your work, marriage, parenting, how are you responding to the one who was crucified so that you could live?

POINTS TO PONDER

> How are you living out your commitment to faith? (Titus 2:11-12).

> How does Romans 6:6 express your new spiritual direction or motivation in light of Jesus' substitution for your sins?

> To what degree is the "life you now live" a reflection of the immensity of Christ's generous exchange (He gave Himself up for me)? (Galatians 2:20b).

34 /

Justice, Mercy & Humility

"He has told you, O man, what is good;
And what does the LORD require of you
But to do justice, to love kindness,
And to walk humbly with your God?"
(Micah 6:8, NASB).

How does God speak justice, mercy and humility to you? The issue of Micah 6:8 was that God's people wanted to know how to placate God (Micah 6:6-7). They seemingly wanted to offer Him what did not require a change of heart or compassion on their part. God rejected their offer of materialism and issued His precise requirements of man: to do justice, to love mercy and to be humble. Service done in God's name is best received when done with a compassionate heart and sincere concern.

The people of Micah's day erred through ingratitude to God, religious pretense, dishonesty, idolatry and the like. The same could be said for the sin of choice today. In view of God's requirement for justice, mercy, and humility, what does it mean to practice these on a daily basis at home and on the job? Within the confines of a close knit, selfless community, it is not a stretch for leaders and subordinates to express selfless love for those they serve alongside. Let's face it, when a leader goes out of his or her way to ensure compliance with safety directives and take extra steps to discourage illegal or potentially harmful behavior, that leader is not only practicing justice but is also demonstrating love and sincere concern. The practice of upholding standards discourages one from straying, thus avoiding unwanted consequences. Humility helps the servant leader find balance between justice and mercy.

The reminder of God's requirements to do justice, love kindness and to walk humbly with Him suggests that the people were doing the opposite.

Consider the opposing actions to his instructions: lack of justice would result in unfair treatment, unreasonableness, and unconcern for others. The opposite of mercy would reflect a lack of compassion, unforgiveness, and unkindness. Absent humility, one becomes prideful, self serving, and arrogantly assertive.

What is God speaking to your heart regarding the application of justice, loving kindness and humility? God's preferred sacrifice is a "broken spirit and a contrite heart" (Psalm 51:17). He rejects self justification but embraces compassion.

POINTS TO PONDER

> What sacrifice of service are you offering God?

> When was the last time your heart was pricked to demonstrate selfless concern for one who did not deserve it?

> Is God pleased with your heart of service?

35 /

Desired End State

"For as many as are the promises of God, in Him they are yes; therefore also through Him is our Amen to the glory of God through us" (2 Corinthians 1:20, NASB).

Spare me the goat trails. Just give me a straight answer! Ever had one of those days when all you wanted was a straight answer? If the Corinthian people ever desired a straight answer, Paul gave it to them. God's promises are "Yes," and the appropriate response is "Amen" (so let it be). There's no gray, no verbal spin, only a matter of fact "Yes." Leaders operate in a fact based realm that sometimes calls for rapid fire decisions. Paul, Silvanus and Timothy preached a fact based gospel (2 Corinthians 1:18-19). In our flesh, so much of what we say is colored with political viewpoints and opinions, but God has not called us to deal in questionable, opinionated answers. His Word is sure and certain. How can we know that His Word is true?

Consider Paul's approach: "When Silas and Timothy came down from Macedonia, Paul began devoting himself completely to the Word, solemnly testifying to the Jews that Jesus was the Christ" (Acts 18:5). Paul's unwavering confidence in the Lord's intent and direction enabled him to speak truth and to move on when his message was rejected (Acts 18:6).

Are you seeking clarity from God on a matter but are uncertain that you are hearing correctly? Here is a thought: Do not ask for something for yourself, but ask that His will in that situation be done and earnestly desire to be part of the answer. God cannot say no to what He has already said yes to.

POINTS TO PONDER

> How do we know the truth? Those who continue in His Word know the truth (John 8:31-32).

> God grants clarity to the concerns of our heart as we spend time with Him and seek His guidance (John 15:7).

> Are you embracing the promises of God, or are you relying on your own understanding? (Proverbs 3:5-6).

36 /

Ready or Not

"Therefore I, the prisoner of the Lord, implore you to walk in a manner worthy of the calling with which you have been called, with all humility and gentleness, with patience, showing tolerance for one another in love" (Ephesians 4:1-2, NASB).

"Ready or not, here I come" announced the start of the hunt in the children's game "Hide and Seek." I could not help but think of that phrase while contemplating Paul's exhortation for Christian unity to the believers in Ephesians 4:1-2. Paul gives a prescription for unity among believers. His ingredients are straightforward: show humility, gentleness, patience, and tolerance through love. Said another way, get along with one another and don't just fake it, show real love. This is how believers walk in a worthy manner. These are qualities true followers of Christ should display.

The challenge for the Christian leader is to live out godlike unity. Paul's instructions to the servant leader are clear as it relates to the workplace believer who is task saturated, the new apprentice, or the anxious co worker. Show gentleness, be compassionate, and practice patience. It is one thing to practice these virtues with believers, but what about our attitude toward the non believer? Are we to display acts of humility, gentleness, patience, and tolerance in love toward all people? Are you ready or not?

Today's cultural challenges require leadership that knows how to deal with recognition of same sex marriage, the impacts of legalization of marijuana use, intimate partner violence episodes, workers whose financial irresponsibility keeps them in arrears in child support payments, to name a few. Tolerance for one another in love does not mean tolerance of all things. Rather, strive to be at peace with one another and speak truth in love in an effort to walk in a manner worthy of Christ's calling.

Ready or Not might be a call to maintain unity of spirit among believers, with a ready a response to help the lost, confused, and misdirected through repentance and renewal in Christ's love. The spiritual leader plants seeds of righteousness. Paul's admonition to "show tolerance for one another in love" is not a call to disregard others' immoral practices, but to be ready to show compassion and to sow seeds of right thinking and being.

POINTS TO PONDER

> How does your compassion identify you as worthy of your calling?

> How might your willingness to breach your comfort zone be the spiritual buoy another needs? (Ephesians 2:10).

> As "His workmanship" (Ephesians 2:10), how might a readiness to teach, coach, or prompt another provide useful options in engaging others where they are?

Monthly Reflection

Monthly Reflection

It's time for a quick evaluation. Use this section to help gauge your habit of integrating faith and profession, and to help get you into the habit of keeping a written record of those times when the Holy Spirit speaks to you. Use the questions below for monthly reflection and to aid a spiritual approach to challenges confronting your application of faith and leadership. The questions are intended for the purpose of self-reflection and contemplation—not guilt and self-loathing.

1. Among your daily requirements, were you able to achieve aside time with God through personal reading of Scripture and prayer?

☐ Yes
☐ No

2. Recall one or two of the most significant leadership challenges you encountered over the past 30 days. What was your response to the challenge(s) and what effect, if any, did your spiritual development priority have on how you addressed the situation?

_____
_____
_____
_____
_____
_____
_____
_____
_____
_____
_____
_____

3. Reflecting over the past 30 days, name one or two ways you met balance between work and family requirements.

_____
_____
_____
_____
_____
_____
_____
_____
_____
_____
_____
_____

4. Have you recently observed an event that you would count as answered prayer?

☐ Yes (explain) _____
_____

☐ No

5. Did you enlist the aid of a prayer partner over the last 30 days?

☐ Yes
☐ No

37 /

Nagging Circumstances

"And he said, 'The LORD has sworn; the LORD will have war against Amalek from generation to generation'" (Exodus 17:16, NASB).

No one desires a persistent enemy. Anyone would be happy for the removal of an irritating thorn in the flesh or for the total eradication of a systemic office problem. The Amalekites may have been a persistent irritation to the Israelites, but who were they to God? They were not a formidable foe for the Lord. For Israel to be in recurring conflict with the Amalekites was certainly better for them than striving against them without the Lord. God's Word to Moses was that He would utterly destroy the Amalekites (Exodus 17:14). Literally and figuratively, God would be in the battle with Israel against their enemy. While Israel would have preferred a less belligerent journey toward the promised land, they would be comforted in God's faithful presence.

Do you find yourself in a persistently problematic circumstance? The leader's challenge usually does not end with conquest over one issue before another arrives. In fact, multiple, simultaneous issues often test a leader's prowess. Our response amid such circumstances should mark us as faithful followers of Christ. Moses availed himself of the help of Aaron and Hur (Exodus 17:10) in battling the Amalekites. Jesus accepted the help of Simon from Cyrene in carrying His cross when He was physically overwhelmed (Mark 15:21). To whom do you turn for help and encouragement when facing a persistent issue?

The Amalekites were not Israel's only enemy, and with the destruction of the Amalekites, God did not cease to be Israel's "banner" (Exodus 17:15). The point is this: God does not abandon us in the face of weighty circumstances and pressures. Consider God's prevailing truth and rely on His presence during your times of need for deliverance from nagging circumstances.

POINTS TO PONDER

> He gives strength for the battle (Exodus 17:13) and rewards courage and skill.

> He brings faithful people alongside us (Exodus 17:12) to help shoulder the burden of our circumstances. Will we strip off pride and accept offers of help?

> Winning a battle does not mean the war is over. Are you confident in God's promise of His abiding presence as you fulfill your leadership responsibilities? (John 14:16).

38 /

Distractions

"So I sent messengers to them, saying, 'I am doing a great work and I cannot come down. Why should the work stop while I leave it and come down to you?'" (Nehemiah 6:3, NASB).

Nehemiah was obviously a man of focus and commitment. It is tough enough working through the routine distractions of a day, not to mention distractions intended to intimidate (Nehemiah 6:1-2). Nehemiah, an unknown newcomer, repeatedly responded with clear resolve not to be drawn or distracted from what he came to town to do, which was to rebuild Jerusalem's wall.

Distractions confront us all. Some distractions are a result of task saturation, simply piling more on our plates than we can reasonably handle. Yet other distractions have influence through other means, such as an unshared vision or fear and intimidation as in the case of Sanballat, Tobiah and Geshem (Nehemiah 6:9, 14). Nehemiah models for us how to respond to distractions and intimidation. Five times Nehemiah refused to turn from what he was called to do. His focus was to complete the great work and not to delay its completion.

Most (especially military) people can appreciate being the new kid on the block, but note how Nehemiah channels any fear, worry, and anxiety. He cried out and asked God to strengthen him (Nehemiah 6:9). He took courage and resisted every ploy of his adversaries. It is naive to think that the work we do in the Lord's name will be received with enthusiasm from everyone. How does one keep focus when distractions and discouragement come? Draw near to God and He will draw near to you. Keep focus on the big picture and ask His help. Remind yourself that what you do is for His glory.

POINTS TO PONDER

> Lack of appreciation by others can lead to untruths about your real effort and motive. It is designed to halt a great work (Nehemiah 6:6, 8).

> Pray about task saturation that can lead to fixation on the surroundings to the exclusion of the goal (Nehemiah 4:9).

> Fear and intimidation are a formidable duo. Rely on the sufficiency of God to equip you for the task (Nehemiah 6:15-16).

Nehemiah and his team completed the wall in 52 days! Fear came upon those who attempted to produce fear in him. Distractions are designed to prevent the great work of God from being completed. Persevere. Have a mind to work (Nehemiah 4:6b). Stay on the wall.

39 /

In His Time

"The LORD your God will clear away these nations before you little by little; you will not be able to put an end to them quickly, for the wild beasts would grow too numerous for you" (Deuteronomy 7:22, NASB).

Even if I want to accomplish something, if it is not God's will, I will not be able to do it. Why would the Lord not allow something that seems a good thing for His people? We most often only perceive what is in front of us, and our tendency is to make decisions based on what we see—the facts. God, on the other hand, has all wisdom, knowledge and understanding and acts according to our best interests, based on more than is apparent to mortal man.

The fact that God will act requires faith and trust on the part of those who look to Him for help. As we trust Him, faith and confidence develop—little by little as we wait with patience. God moves on behalf of those who trust Him. Gradually, the mustard seed germinates and develops into a thriving tree. Draconian actions can overwhelm and negate good intentions. Seeds need time to develop just as the enthusiasm of a new Christian should be channeled to outlets of sound spiritual development.

Little by little, in God's time He performs His purposes. Some leaders, thrust into positions of greater responsibility as a reward for a job well done, fizzle in their performance because they lack the wisdom that seasoning and time bring.

The route to success is through recognition of the One who is really creating the headway: "The LORD your God will." God does the heavy lifting. Joshua could not take credit for his victorious army; God fought for Israel (Joshua 10:42). Our best plan should be to cooperate with God in recognition of our mortal limitations: "You will not be able to put an end to them quickly." Is not our challenge to recognize there is more to matters than what is in front of us? God acts on behalf of those He loves (Deuteronomy 7:12), and He has a wonderful plan for us despite present circumstances.

POINTS TO PONDER

> How are you demonstrating cooperation with God in leadership on the job or in the home?

> Do you trust God to work all things for your good in His time? (Exodus 23:29-30).

> Within our flesh, God's plans are hard to discern; through acts of trust and faith. We come to accept His intentions as good (Jeremiah 29:11).

40 /

The Way Ahead—Choose to Forgive

"For if you forgive others for their transgressions, your heavenly Father will also forgive you. But if you do not forgive others, then your Father will not forgive your transgressions" (Matthew 6:14-15, NASB).

Forgiveness is a choice. If my spouse does something that offends me, I can decide to be hurt, to rehearse the offense in my mind and to allow frustration, anger, and unforgiveness to set in. Conversely, if I keep my wits about me and follow Jesus' instructions, I will choose to forgive and move on. Peter asked, "How often should I forgive?" (Matthew 18:21). Not knowing to forgive is not the issue; choosing to forgive hits at the heart of the struggle. Jesus instructs us not to withhold forgiveness, but to freely forgive.

What about forgiveness in the workplace? Is forgiveness measured out by good or bad performance? Too many headlines read like this: Commander Jones was relieved of his duties because leaders lost confidence in his ability to effectively lead and perform assigned duties. There is no question leaders have a responsibility to uphold workplace performance standards and maintain good order and discipline. Consequences properly follow violations, but Jesus' admonition to forgive also pertains to workplace justice. Marginalizing or devaluing one who has erred or denying such a one a path to restoration of workplace fellowship is not Christ's brand of forgiveness. Leadership fosters growth out of genuine value placed on each person.

It is best to let the mind of Christ guide workplace forgiveness and restoration acts. I almost erred by allowing a worker's prior disciplined misstep to determine whether I would hire this person. A decision not to hire her would have meant that a less qualified person would have been selected for the position. As I asked the person about her previous infraction, she said to me, "At some point someone has to give me a chance." The fact is, she had suffered the consequences several times over for her mistake, and I was in a position to make her pay once more. Forgiveness is a life restoring, healing act, extended in obedience to Jesus' teachings and His examples. That hiring decision turned out to be one of my best actions as the worker became a highly responsible top performer. Whether in a personal relationship or in the workplace, Jesus' admonition to forgive remains. As servant leaders, how we forgive and restore is a mark of obedience to Christ's commands.

POINTS TO PONDER

> Turn anger and hot emotions over to God as an expression of godly character and with an earnest desire for the best for others (2 Corinthians 2:7).

> Do what God has instructed and trust Him for the results. Take every thought captive to the knowledge of Christ (2 Corinthians 10:5).

> Exercise responsible leadership by maintaining good order and discipline but refrain from devaluing one who has come under discipline.

Monthly Reflection

Monthly Reflection

It's time for a quick evaluation. Use this section to help gauge your habit of integrating faith and profession, and to help get you into the habit of keeping a written record of those times when the Holy Spirit speaks to you. Use the questions below for monthly reflection and to aid a spiritual approach to challenges confronting your application of faith and leadership. The questions are intended for the purpose of self-reflection and contemplation—not guilt and self-loathing.

1. Among your daily requirements, were you able to achieve aside time with God through personal reading of Scripture and prayer?

☐ Yes
☐ No

2. Recall one or two of the most significant leadership challenges you encountered over the past 30 days. What was your response to the challenge(s) and what effect, if any, did your spiritual development priority have on how you addressed the situation?

_____
_____
_____
_____
_____
_____
_____
_____
_____

3. Reflecting over the past 30 days, name one or two ways you met balance between work and family requirements.

4. Have you recently observed an event that you would count as answered prayer?

☐ Yes (explain)

☐ No

5. Did you enlist the aid of a prayer partner over the last 30 days?

☐ Yes
☐ No

41 /

Unintended Consequences

"Then Satan stood up against Israel and moved David to number Israel" (1 Chronicles 21:1, NASB).

Have you ever been checked in your spirit to rectify an ill advised decision that disregarded unintended consequences, but you pushed ahead with it anyway? I know I have, and so did David. In spite of rational counsel by David's most trusted leader and warrior, David did not change his decision to conduct a census to determine the number of Israelite citizens under his leadership (1 Chronicles 21:3). David's action was not only displeasing to Joab, but it also displeased God (1 Chronicles 21:7).

When you know you have created a mess, how do you reverse it? Here's an answer—follow David's example. Humble yourself, repent, and submit to God. When forcing a short sighted decision, perhaps what is really happening is the lust of the flesh rebelling against the divine promptings of the Holy Spirit's guidance: "Your ears will hear a word behind you, 'This is the way, walk in it,' whenever you turn to the right or to the left" (Isaiah 30:21). Most decisions have consequences, and David was in great distress over the unintended consequences his decision had brought on his nation (1 Chronicles 21:8). His foolish actions resulted in 70,000 slain and created the real possibility of additional death and destruction had the Lord not halted the full consequences. David repented of his sin and appealed to God for mercy (1 Chronicles 21:8, 17).

Does David's rash act resonate with you? Have you made an error in judgment by insisting things go your way? Perhaps you are presently in the midst of unintended consequences from a rash decision. If so, follow David's example.

POINTS TO PONDER

> Humbly admit your sin and take responsibility for the role you played (1 Chronicles 21:8).

> Commend and trust yourself to the hands of a merciful God who is concerned for you and for those He has entrusted to you (1 Chronicles 21:13).

> Adjust your course and get back on track with the heart of a servant leader, putting the needs of others ahead of your own (1 Chronicles 21:17).

42 /

The Preeminent God

"So I spoke to the people in the morning, and in the evening my wife died. And in the morning I did as I was commanded" (Ezekiel 24:18, NASB).

How hard is it to be stripped of one's most valued possession and be denied grieving rights? God's relationship with his prophets often defied comprehension. Using them as object lessons in some instances, He asked them to consider obedience of greater importance than even their personal lives. Ezekiel's commitment and obedience to God are highlighted in a most provocative way. The prophet was to know in advance that his wife would die that day and was to refrain from mourning her. What a struggle it would be to perform one's duties following a spouse's demise without betraying the emotion of loss for the one who was "his great delight." What did God want from Ezekiel? Could God's response to the declaration of Samaria and Jerusalem's adultery and idolatry not be portrayed in a less intrusive manner?

Much can be learned from Ezekiel's response. He did not question or bargain with God. Why? Ezekiel was convinced of God's preeminence in much the same way as Abraham who declared of God, "He can raise him from the dead," when he lifted the knife to take Isaac's life. To Ezekiel, God's preeminence—his first place in judging, offering up for destruction, or extending mercy—did not diminish at the door of personal sacrifice. He was the Lord's prophet, accustomed to knowing God's mind and will for the people before the events took place. He had pledged faithful service and determined to get to the end of his service with his integrity in tact. After all, the message he delivered would be compromised by a lesser commitment.

The people prized the temple and its activity over the Lord Himself, and God was preparing to strip it away from them. Their lack of regard for His holiness flew in the face of His jealous claim on the whole heart of the people (Ezekiel 23:36-39). In what ways do we demonstrate this same carelessness? What gives you greater delight—loyalty to a program, an institution, a promotion, or obedience to God? God has not asked for the sacrifice of the family or called for slackness on the job as demonstration of commitment to Him. God took Ezekiel's wife as sign of the reverence and obedience He required of His people. God wants the acknowledged, preeminent position in each of our lives.

POINTS TO PONDER

> Is there "a delight" in your life that surpasses your reverence for God? (Ezekiel 24:25).

> Has the work of your hands become your sanctuary, full of pride and desire? (Ezekiel 24:21).

> And in the morning I did as I was commanded. Are you able to let go of the temporal for the eternal good God wants to perform through you?

43 /

Seeing the Other Side

"But I have prayed for you, that your faith may not fail; and you, when once you have turned again, strengthen your brothers" (Luke 22:32, NASB).

When all seems against you and you are hard pressed to get others to perform at a higher standard, what do you do?

The cross looming large before Him, Jesus, perhaps, had a similar concern. What was His approach to changing complacency, shallow commitment, and naïve vulnerability? Prayer! Anyone who chooses to follow Jesus' path will be a clear and discernable target of Satan. Simon did not realize the target he had become (Luke 22:31). He also could not imagine that he would abandon Jesus out of fear for his personal comfort or loss of life. When pushed to hold to the integrity he professed (Luke 22:33-34), Peter would cave. Jesus prayed that on the other side of his failure Peter would turn towards the lessons he learned and be an encouragement to his brothers.

Often in difficulties, it is hard to believe that anything worthwhile lies on the other side of disobedience, dereliction, self satisfaction, or marginal commitment. Jesus desired that passion for service (Luke 22:27) be ignited in His followers. So how does one stimulate fervor for service in a person who is oblivious to the greater good or bigger picture? Within ourselves, we cannot. I consider inspiration to be a "God breathed" phenomena. However, we can intercede for others and credit God for answering our prayer on another's behalf. Peter did not understand failure until he publically denied Jesus. He would only become an encouraging example for his brothers because of Jesus' prayers for him.

For many the backside of disobedience, waywardness, and complacency is ruin and disappointment. Sometimes, no words or warnings will deter a person from doing the wrong thing. Jesus did not attempt to dissuade Simon from his approaching denial. Consider that our leadership role is not always one of preventing another from his determined path. In some cases, the correction or consequence that follows will have the greater impact on a person's decision to walk with integrity. Jesus modeled the classic response to develop passion in others. Pray.

POINTS TO PONDER

> Desire for greatness or prominence must be tempered with a servant's heart (Luke 22:26-27).

> Prayer should be the foundation of our concern for others (Luke 22:32).

> Failure need not equate to disqualification from the cause nor interpreted as an inability to help and encourage others (Luke 22:32).

44 /

Compassion

"Should I not have compassion on Nineveh, the great city in which there are more than 120,000 persons who do not know the difference between their right and left hand, as well as many animals?" (Jonah 4:11, NASB).

Compassion, a selfless concern or kind regard for the welfare of another, is a much needed grace in short supply in our world. Something that should be freely given, compassion is often wielded as a weapon withheld to control others or as a reward for good behavior. A compassionate person is authentically encouraging. Jonah interpreted the mercy and compassion of God (Jonah 4:2) as weakness toward sinful Nineveh.

Jonah was called by God to encourage the people of Nineveh to turn from their sins. He was to preach against Nineveh, so they would turn to God and away from the destruction they deserved. After a false start in the wrong direction, Jonah did encourage the people (Jonah 3:4) by stating, "Yet forty days and Nineveh will be overthrown." How is that for encouragement? Nonetheless, the people and the king repented in response to Jonah's compassionless proclamation. Jonah was displeased and angry (Jonah 4:1). Where was his compassion for the people?

It is hard to read the story of Jonah and not examine my own feelings or actions of bigotry. God showed compassion to the ignorant Ninevites in their repentant state. I have to admit that, like Jonah, I don't always want to show compassion. I would rather make another's good behavior a precondition for my compassion. God also had a precondition for Nineveh, but His motives were far more pure than mine would ever be. God took note of the number of people in that city, and He pointed out their ignorance—they do not know the difference between their right and left hand.

What might have caused Jonah to withhold compassion? What might cause you to be stingy with empathy or sympathy? Few things are worse than arrogance. Are you tempted to make your compassion for others conditional? Jonah mishandled conditional compassion and revealed his own judgmental and prideful arrogance. Let us strive to find the right blend of Christ filled compassion and Spirit guided correction.

POINTS TO PONDER

> Is the salvation of others, regardless of their sin, a priority to you? (Romans 6:23).

> Would your family or coworkers characterize you as a compassionate person?

> What does your compassion look like in the home? At work? (James 2:13, 5:11).

45 /

Did You Ask?

"So Saul died for his trespass which he committed against the LORD, because of the word of the LORD which he did not keep; and also because he asked counsel of a medium, making inquiry of it, and did not inquire of the LORD. Therefore He killed him and turned the kingdom to David the son of Jesse" (1 Chronicles 10:13-14, NASB).

"You didn't ask!" Perhaps someone has made that retort to you when you finally came around to finding "the right question" to your question. Possibly, you have found yourself on the delivery end of that statement.

Saul, Israel's first king, turned to the wrong source when his heart overruled the sound, Spirit directed guidance he should have sought. Instead of turning to God who established him as king, he turned to a spiritist or fortune teller for direction. Saul failed to present himself to God, choosing rather to put his trust in man's counsel. Consequently, he lost his kingdom and his life. Not his first lapse in judgment in this area, Saul may have succumbed to the proverbial "If you can't stand the answer, don't ask the question." Because he refused to know God's heart, Saul lost his life.

God's first requirement is obedience (1 Samuel 15:22). It offends God when we turn from "obedience to his voice" to other means of direction. He is jealous for our loyalty. Consider a spouse asking a neighbor to do something her husband was well qualified to do but not given the chance to accomplish. Understandably, the husband's jealousy meter would be off the chart. Honestly, we may not always know the right question to ask or the best person to address a concern. That, however, was not the case with Saul, who died because he did not keep the word God had given him. Saul's willful disobedience prompts the questions: Have you done the last thing God asked you to do? Did you understand the tasking, or do you need to return to Him for direction or clarification?

From whom do you seek advice and in whom do you place your trust when it seems you are not receiving discernable direction from God? Asking counsel of wise people is a Scriptural response, and so is asking God to keep you from presumption (Psalm 19:12-13). To presume is to say, "I know best. I do not need to ask God." Not seeking God's heart will not excuse you.

POINTS TO PONDER

The Scripture speaks volumes about seeking counsel and sound wisdom:

> Proverbs 3:5-6 warns against depending on one's own understanding.

> Psalm 119:24 states that the Scriptures are delightful counselors. Allow God's Word, precepts, and instructions to be your "go to" source.

> James 1:5 encourages, "If any of you lacks wisdom, he should ask God." Will you ask God first and allow Him to point you in the right direction?

Monthly Reflection

Monthly Reflection

It's time for a quick evaluation. Use this section to help gauge your habit of integrating faith and profession, and to help get you into the habit of keeping a written record of those times when the Holy Spirit speaks to you. Use the questions below for monthly reflection and to aid a spiritual approach to challenges confronting your application of faith and leadership. The questions are intended for the purpose of self-reflection and contemplation—not guilt and self-loathing.

1. Among your daily requirements, were you able to achieve aside time with God through personal reading of Scripture and prayer?

☐ Yes
☐ No

2. Recall one or two of the most significant leadership challenges you encountered over the past 30 days. What was your response to the challenge(s) and what effect, if any, did your spiritual development priority have on how you addressed the situation?

_____
_____
_____
_____
_____
_____
_____
_____
_____
_____

3. Reflecting over the past 30 days, name one or two ways you met balance between work and family requirements.

4. Have you recently observed an event that you would count as answered prayer?

☐ Yes (explain)

☐ No

5. Did you enlist the aid of a prayer partner over the last 30 days?

☐ Yes
☐ No

46 /

Transformation: Clean the Root and Reinsert It

"I find then the principle that evil is present in me, the one who wants to do good" (Romans 7:21, NASB).

Dig through the dirt, go deep, clear everything out of the way, find the root, grab it, clean it, and, with great care, replant the root. Transformation starts when we, in cooperation with God, strip away veneer and fully expose to God a heart in need of His cultivation. Having entrusted to God areas of vulnerabilities, put into place spiritual practices that will resist re introduction of the old nature.

How different are we from the writer of Romans? Paul stated so eloquently the dual nature of the fleshly struggle: But if I am doing the very thing I do not want, I am no longer the one doing it, but sin which dwells in me (Romans 7:20). Transformation starts with God, and with no less power will the influence of the flesh be defeated. Recently, a guy shared with me that he and his wife experienced spiritual milestones on the same day. He rededicated his life to Christ, and she participated in believer's baptism. What a delight it was for the two of them! He said that now people ask, "Why do you attend two Bible studies during the week, in addition to attending worship services on Sunday?" His response displays credit to the work of transformation taking place in his life. He states earnestly, "I need to. It keeps me from returning to bad habits, and besides," he added, "all I would otherwise be doing is watching TV."

How do we overcome the dueling natures, the struggle of the flesh to do evil and of the mind that knows to obey the commands of God? We clear away the debris and cultivate in our heart the mind of Christ.

POINTS TO PONDER

Consider these leadership challenges as indications that transformation is occurring:

> Tightness in the chest is replaced by soft responses. "A gentle answer turns away wrath…" (Proverbs 15:1a).

> Disagreements are toned down and extending grace becomes an easier alternative. "Let your speech always be with grace, as though seasoned with salt, so that you will know how you should respond to each person" (Colossians 4:6).

> Blaming others for our personal shortcomings is replaced with ownership and responsibility for personal spiritual growth. "First take the log out of your own eye, and then you will see clearly to take out the speck that is in your brother's eye" (Luke 6:42b).

47 /

The Right Heart

"When the bow is in the cloud, then I will look upon it, to remember the everlasting covenant between God and every living creature of all flesh that is on the earth" (Genesis 9:16, NASB).

Not all covenants are unrestricted, but God's covenant with Noah was unconditional. God keeps His covenant independent of man's obedience. God will do what He says He will do—this covenant with man is, in fact, one-sided. After nearly twelve months of water completely covering the earth, God's wrath was satisfied. He cleansed the earth and purged wicked man from it (Genesis 8:13-14). Though God cleansed the earth of man, He did not cleanse man's heart (Genesis 8:21). Why?

God is after something here. Man's free will love and obedience was his desire in the garden and in giving his commands to Israel through Moses (Deuteronomy 6:4-6). Loving obedience to God is within man's reach. Noah found favor in God's eyes, as one who was righteous and without blame (Genesis 6:8-9). Whatever motivated God's covenanting with man must also inspire His love for man. When we choose God, He is pleased. God did not command Noah's worship or his burnt offering upon returning to dry land, but God was pleased to receive his worship and was soothed by its pleasant aroma (Genesis 8:20-21).

God desires our unprovoked worship and obedience. God absolutely loves it when we turn to Him and worship Him with a heart that says: "Not my will, but your will be done." God initiates unqualified covenant because though the "intent of man's heart is evil," not everyone lives out the evil intent—though provoked. For ten righteous men God spares a city (Genesis 18:32). God is pleased with the heart of a righteous person (James 5:16).

What is the condition of your heart? When all around you succumb to evil intent, do you hold to the narrow way and find God's favor? Being an effective leader is as much about having the right heart as following proven leadership practices. God covenants with man and He always keeps His Word.

POINTS TO PONDER

> Consider how you commit your ways to God (Proverbs 3:5-6).

> How are you resisting when all around are caving to common cultural demands or political correctness? (James 4:7).

> Keep doing the right thing, even when it is unpopular (Proverbs 28:20).

48 /

Daniel's Wise Alternative

"But Daniel made up his mind that he would not defile himself with the king's choice food or with the wine which he drank; so he sought permission from the commander of the officials that he might not defile himself" (Daniel 1:8, NASB).

Born in the 1880s, William Borden was the son of the notable producer of Borden's dairy products. Responding to the call of Christ on his life. William renounced his life of affluence and traveled to Egypt to prepare for the mission field. He contracted meningitis in Egypt and died at the age of 25. Later, his parents found in his Bible the words "No Reserves," dated shortly after he rejected fortune in favor of missions. In another place in his Bible he had written "No Retreat," dated after his father told him he would never work for the Borden Company again. Shortly before he died in Egypt, he added the phrase "No Regrets." Those six words defined young William Borden's life resolve: "No reserves, no retreat, no regrets."

Daniel lived his life with similar resolve toward God as did William Borden. At a young age (some estimate twelve to fourteen), Daniel was taken captive and placed in service in Babylon under Nebuchadnezzar's rule. When confronted with assuming a Babylonian diet of food forbidden by his scriptural teachings (Leviticus 11:2-8), Daniel declared he would not defile himself with the king's choice food and wine (Daniel 1:8). Instead, he asked for vegetables and water in place of the king's food and wine.

What will loyalty and faithfulness to God get you? In Daniel's case, first, it got him the favor and compassion of his chief training official. Daniel made his declaration not to defile himself with an alternate plan in mind. Though a youth, Daniel's request reflected his trainer's concern that he not lose his life by compromising his responsibility to assimilate Daniel and his three friends into the Babylonian culture (Daniel 1:10). Daniel did not stage a hunger strike. He asked that they be given vegetables and water for ten days followed by comparison with the other youth in appearance and training (Daniel 1:12-13). Daniel's request was reasonable and his trainer agreed to the trial.

Daniel's loyalty and faithfulness to God also netted him a host of knowledge, intellect, wisdom, and the ability to understand visions and dreams (Daniel 1:17). God did not stop there. Daniel and his friends' loyalty to God resulted in an audience with Babylon's decision maker, King Nebuchadnezzar. Nebuchadnezzar observed the wisdom and understanding of Daniel and his friends and found them ten times better than all the magicians and conjurers who were in all of his realm (Daniel 1:20).

Though efforts may be taken to change one's worldview, believers must decide on Scriptural hotspots or points of no compromise and maintain faithfulness to God. Daniel's resolve helped him to discern a wise, alternate plan. Christ followers can expect to "...hear a word behind you, saying: 'This is the way, walk in it, whenever you turn to the right hand or whenever you turn to the left'" (Isaiah 30:21). Doubtless, Daniel's wise request was in response to hearing God through prayer and study of the Scriptures.

Discerning wisdom is not an overnight process. Spiritual wisdom accompanies the practice of spiritual disciplines, particularly when prayer and Bible study are hallmarks. Daniel's practice of spiritual disciplines (Daniel 6:10) readied him with a wise response when his circumstances demanded compromise (Daniel 9:2-3).

POINTS TO PONDER

> Are there cultural issues that you defend or reject which oppose God's clear teaching? Consider that, like Daniel, you may be assuming responsibility for other believers under your influence (Daniel 1:11-12).

> How do you respond when you feel your "rights" have been violated? Are you willing to give up your rights for the good of someone else? (Philippians 2:3-4).

> In what areas of faith have you declared, "No reserves, no retreat, no regrets?"

49 /

Character of a Leader—Holy?

"And one called out to another and said, 'Holy, Holy, Holy, is the LORD of hosts, the whole earth is full of His glory'" (Isaiah 6:3, NASB).

Have you considered holiness as an essential leadership quality? I have to admit, when I think of leadership essentials, "holy" does not immediately surface as a necessary trait. What comes to mind when you hear the word "holy?" "Holy roller" and "holier than thou" are cultural expressions we hear. Sadly, the tendency is to use "holy" in a derogatory sense. In his book *Leadership Essentials*, Greg Ogden makes the point, "The Bible is much more concerned about who a leader is than what a leader does." That is similar to his thought, "Developing character is more important than polishing skills." Performance is the usual bottom line indicator and bread and butter for leaders. However, how are Christ's followers to be as servant leaders?

What does it mean to be holy? Jesus is the perfect model of holiness. Based on His life, holiness would include the absence of sin and the presence of fruit of the Spirit. Jesus knew no sin. However, because we are sinful, yet chosen to carry out God's work on earth, it is useful to recount Isaiah's entry into the service of God. Read Isaiah 6:1-8. Isaiah decried his sin before a holy God, saying: "I am a man of unclean lips, and I live among a people of unclean lips" (Isaiah 6:5). With a "live coal" Isaiah's lips were touched, his guilt was taken away, and his sin atoned for (Isaiah 6:6-7). We, as Isaiah, have not lived sinless lives, but through forgiveness of sin, the Lord used Isaiah and uses us in spiritual service. Holiness is purity. Though sinful, the one who confesses his sin is purified for service.

Finally, as disciples of Christ we should follow His example and exhibit the Spirit's fruit (Galatians 5:22-23). What good news! When the Spirit of God leads our hearts, good fruit is the result, and the sin nature is quelled. The fruit of the Spirit is love, joy, peace, patience, kindness, goodness, faithfulness, gentleness and self-control. These qualities abounded in Jesus. As disciples called to lead, we are made to have His nature.

Take a minute and evaluate the presence of the fruit of the Spirit in your life. Which fruit is most abundant in your life right now? After reflecting on the abundance, think on the fruit you sense needs to be growing in you.

POINTS TO PONDER

Consider these ways to cultivate greater abundance of the Spirit's fruit:

> Offer a prayer to God to help your weakness become your strength (Philippians 4:6).

> Following periods of Bible reading, journal over the next seven days. What applications are the Holy Spirit revealing concerning the fruit you desire in greater abundance (Proverbs 3:5-6).

> What God has given in abundance, use to His glory. Let our strengths honor Him (Galatians 5:25).

Monthly Reflection

Monthly Reflection

It's time for a quick evaluation. Use this section to help gauge your habit of integrating faith and profession, and to help get you into the habit of keeping a written record of those times when the Holy Spirit speaks to you. Use the questions below for monthly reflection and to aid a spiritual approach to challenges confronting your application of faith and leadership. The questions are intended for the purpose of self-reflection and contemplation—not guilt and self-loathing.

1. Among your daily requirements, were you able to achieve aside time with God through personal reading of Scripture and prayer?

☐ Yes
☐ No

2. Recall one or two of the most significant leadership challenges you encountered over the past 30 days. What was your response to the challenge(s) and what effect, if any, did your spiritual development priority have on how you addressed the situation?

_____
_____
_____
_____
_____
_____
_____
_____
_____

3. Reflecting over the past 30 days, name one or two ways you met balance between work and family requirements.

_____
_____
_____
_____
_____
_____
_____
_____
_____
_____
_____
_____

4. Have you recently observed an event that you would count as answered prayer?

☐ Yes (explain) _____
_____

☐ No

5. Did you enlist the aid of a prayer partner over the last 30 days?

☐ Yes
☐ No

50 /

Discouragement—I Have Had Enough!

"While He himself went a day's journey into the wilderness. He came to a broom bush, sat down under it and prayed that he might die. 'I have had enough, LORD,' he said. 'Take my life; I am no better than my ancestors'" (1 Kings 19:4, NIV).

Discouragement. Is there anything worse? Discouragement can suck the life out of momentum and halt forward progress. It has been stated that following victory discouragement and compromise can ensue. Elijah, God's messenger to Ahab (1 Kings 18:1), experienced a decisive victory over Ahab's prophets of Baal at Mount Carmel (1 Kings 18:16 40), but on the heels of victory he found himself far opposite God's intention. What could have caused Elijah to move so quickly from God's will? Fear and discouragement from a well timed threat (1 Kings 19:3, 10) made Elijah throw it in reverse and flee for his life. Wandering off in the desert, discouraged and desirous of death, he abandoned his helper and concluded that he was the lone survivor of those interested in the things of God. If mishandled, discouragement can take us off task, produce feelings of aloneness and cloud our judgment.

Can you recall a time when you reacted to a situation from raw, fearful emotion rather than by seeking God's comfort? Elijah would rather have faced death than the threat of his life being taken. God revealed Himself to Elijah with this question: "What are you doing here?" (1 Kings 19:9). Isolation is often the enemy of a courageous response. Not even the strongest earthquake will free us from its grip. Discouragement can place us at opposite ends of God's intention requiring Him to correct us, turn us around, and put us back on His course. God told Elijah to go back the way he came (1 Kings 19:15).

Sometimes we can feel that we have had enough. Truthfully, if God has called us to a task, He will be the one to determine when He is done using us. Discouragement will be there despite the truth. Elijah felt alone—he was not! (1 Kings 19:18) He did not know the truth of God's plan. Don't allow threats or the appearance of being the only one interested in what God is working halt your forward momentum and progress.

POINTS TO PONDER

> Recognize that believers can and do experience spiritual highs and lows. Avoid course redirection, especially when God mapped the course (1 Peter 5:7).

> Pray—ask God's help in seeing beyond the range of natural thinking, limited perspective, and dulled spiritual insight (2 Kings 6:15-17).

> Be open to the possibility that God reveals Himself in unexpected ways and sometimes through a "gentle whisper" (1 Kings 19:12 and Isaiah 30:21).

51 /

Where Now is the Lord?

"He took the cloak that had fallen from Elijah and struck the water with it. 'Where now is the LORD, the God of Elijah?' he asked. When he struck the water, it divided to the right and to the left, and he crossed over" (2 Kings 2:14, NIV).

Elisha's master had just been whisked away in a "chariot of fire with horses of fire." Many who witnessed his departure also knew that Elisha was the appointed successor (1 Kings 19:19). The same tender, young man who could not follow Elijah until he "kissed his father and mother" goodbye now grieves Elijah's "home going" by tearing his clothing. His comment "My father! My father! The chariots and horsemen of Israel" might suggest that young Elisha comprehends the gravity of the post he has inherited. As he strikes the Jordan River with Elijah's cloak, he asks, "Where now is the LORD, the God of Elijah?" He uses his master's cloak to demonstrate that his request for a double portion of Elijah's spirit had been granted him.

Was it arrogance for the young man to ask for a double portion? Apparently, two shares or a double portion was an indicator of legitimate succession. The sons of the Jericho prophets witness this miracle and declare, "The spirit of Elijah rests on Elisha" (2 Kings 2:15).

Imitation is said to be the greatest form of flattery. What a winsome testimony when a son emulates the godly leadership of his father or a young officer that of a leader of integrity! Elisha had seen in Elijah characteristics worthy of emulation in a nation ruled largely by godless kings. The power of God was strong in the life of Elijah, and Elisha desired the presence of his teacher's teacher. Striking the ground as he had seen Elijah do, he cried out: "Where now is the LORD?" When circumstances turn from desirable to undesirable or when the task ahead is greater than one's resources, it is common to want to know our importance to God and whether He is with us in our labors. We are not all like Elisha, who had a fire of faith blazing in him, emboldening him to ask for a double portion. If, like Elisha, you have made an abrupt life style change to follow God (1 Kings 19:21), you may find yourself asking if this is really His plan for you. If you were Elisha striking the Jordan, you might have asked: "Will God be as faithful to me as He was to Elijah?"

POINTS TO PONDER

> Elisha knew God was with him. How do you know whether God is with you? (Hebrews 13:5).

> Elisha asked for a double portion. Is it appropriate to ask God for big things? Is something burning in you to accomplish for God? (Ephesians 3:20).

> Elisha had a godly mentor or teacher. Are you going it alone? (2 Timothy 1:2-6).

> Elijah identified a successor to the important work. Whom are you bringing along in faith, profession, or relationships? (2 Timothy 2:1-2).

52 /

Rest Interrupted—Reasonable Work/Rest Rhythm

"And He said to them, 'Come away by yourselves to a secluded place and rest a while.' (For there were many people coming and going, and they did not even have time to eat.)" (Mark 6:31, NASB).

What would you consider a reasonable work/rest rhythm? In Mark 6:7-13, 30-32, and 33-46, Jesus models the dynamics of work and rest. Having sent His disciples on mission to preach repentance, cast out demons, and anoint and heal the sick, He told them to "come away" and rest. Rest has obvious benefits, but sometimes we must be told to rest. The disciples "gathered together with Jesus and reported to Him all they had done and taught." Stopping to appreciate our accomplishments is a good thing; we get to check an item off our "to do" list and to enjoy the feeling of positive reinforcement. However, before Jesus and the disciples would embark upon the next task, Jesus wanted them to come aside to a secluded place for rest. Coming in many forms, rest helps to us recover and to be ready for the mission that will surely follow.

What does rest look like for you? For some, it is "sleeping in" with total disregard for time, watching a Sunday afternoon game with feet elevated—drifting in and out of consciousness, working in the garden, or sitting on the porch thinking about nothing. Another form of rest is quiet time with the Lord, resting in the comfort of His Word and releasing all concerns to His care. Rest gives us a better response to trials, stresses and difficulties.

Accomplishments are important, but so are rest and balance that ready us for the next thing. Jesus' admonition to rest is important because rest helps sustain us for the long haul. We never know what is around the corner, and, as Mark 6:33-34 indicates, another opportunity for work awaited them at the secluded place. Where the disciples thought they would have a time of rest alone with Jesus, it did not quite turn out that way. The presence of the crowd presents an important question: How do you respond to interruptions?

Jesus and the disciples expected to arrive at a secluded place for rest. However, "when Jesus went ashore, He saw a large crowd" (Mark 6:34). We can learn much from Jesus' response to this interruption. "He felt compassion for them because they were like sheep without a shepherd; and He began to teach them many things." Interruptions can be opportunities to demonstrate compassion. Jesus' compassion included serving the crowd a meal (Mark 6:35-44). How we respond when our plans get changed can add to or take away from our resilience. The disciples' resilience was not minimized by the interruption. Jesus' response ensured their staying power would be maximized.

The interruption did not remove Jesus' need for rest. Like an accommodating host, Jesus took responsibility for the crowd and sent the disciples on their way to rest. After the crowd was gone, Jesus retreated alone to the mountain to pray, remaining true to His own call for rest. How does Jesus response to this interruption encourage you?

POINTS TO PONDER

Consider your own work/rest rhythm and answer YES or NO to these questions:

> Am I allowing margin between activities?

> Am I practicing balance in apportioning my time?

> Do my margin and balance conform to my family's or my personal priorities?

> If unable to "come away," do I need to rethink in whom or what I am I placing my trust?

> Do I believe success or failure is on my shoulders alone?

53 /

He Will Be With You

"But Moses said to God, 'Who am I that I should go to Pharaoh and bring the Israelites out of Egypt?' And God said, 'I will be with you'" (Exodus 3:11-12a, NIV).

Recall a time you were faced with a difficult task—personally, professionally, or relationally. Did you doubt that you could pull off the seemingly impossible, made dubious not due to elements of the assignment but because of the overwhelming courage or faith it would require?

Many men and women of faith have encountered such mountainous, faith-defining missions. As Moses was given his tasking, he was fully aware that neither escaping Egypt nor acquiring the land that flowed with "milk and honey" would be easy (Exodus 3:7-10). New to his relationship with God (whose name he did not yet know), Moses is being asked to return to the place and person he had fled in fear of his life. Further, he would have to deliver a face-to-face message that would not be received well. Whatever his many apprehensions, the insufficiency of his speech, and the deafening pounding of his heart, God calmed Moses with these words: "I will be with you."

Wow! God's words were designed to give Moses confidence for the road ahead. What would Moses do with the assurance of God's presence? What have you done with His assurance? I have done better at some times than at others. When it comes to integrating the Christian faith with profession, the point of reliance for mission accomplishment is on the One who says, "I will be with you." We know the end of Moses' story and the daunting tasks he faced all along the road to success, but God's promise stood firm. He never left Moses.

Another young man, Gideon, was called to "Go in the strength you have and save Israel out of Midian's hand" (Judges 6:14a). Like Moses he had a list of protests or reasons why he was surely not the one God was now choosing. To this the Lord's response was "I will be with you" (Judges 6:16). Through the Angel of the Lord, the God of Israel had already expressed faith in him and promised his presence: "The Lord is with you, mighty warrior" (Judges 6:12). After a series of displays—an offering consumed on a rock and two fleece tests—Gideon steps out in faith and obeys God's call. God was sending Gideon, and Gideon was going forward.

What about you? Do you sense God calling you out, asking you to do something that is outside your comfort zone? What is your source of strength? Moses asked if another could take his place, but God sent his brother Aaron to help him. God recognized Gideon's fear and told him he could take his servant Purah (Judges 7:10) with him to discover strength for his daunting task. In your intimidating assignment look for encouragement through a prayer partner, a mentoring relationship, or participation in a workplace Bible study.

POINTS TO PONDER

Here are some faith builders to help us know God is with us in every task:

> Exercise awareness that God desires to act through the faithful (2 Chronicles 16:9).

> See faith as a verb. Move out in response to what you know God is asking of you (Romans 1:17).

> Come alongside others. Your active faith bolsters the courage of others who may be facing similar challenges (1 Thessalonians 5:11).

Monthly Reflection

Monthly Reflection

It's time for a quick evaluation. Use this section to help gauge your habit of integrating faith and profession, and to help get you into the habit of keeping a written record of those times when the Holy Spirit speaks to you. Use the questions below for monthly reflection and to aid a spiritual approach to challenges confronting your application of faith and leadership. The questions are intended for the purpose of self-reflection and contemplation—not guilt and self-loathing.

1. Among your daily requirements, were you able to achieve aside time with God through personal reading of Scripture and prayer?

☐ Yes
☐ No

2. Recall one or two of the most significant leadership challenges you encountered over the past 30 days. What was your response to the challenge(s) and what effect, if any, did your spiritual development priority have on how you addressed the situation?

3. Reflecting over the past 30 days, name one or two ways you met balance between work and family requirements.

4. Have you recently observed an event that you would count as answered prayer?

☐ Yes (explain)

☐ No

5. Did you enlist the aid of a prayer partner over the last 30 days?

☐ Yes
☐ No

"But it is good for me to draw near to God: I have put my trust in the Lord God, that I may declare all thy works."
Psalm 73:28 (KJV)

OFFICERS' CHRISTIAN FELLOWSHIP
Building Christian leaders, families, fellowships...*for a lifetime*

About OCF

Officers' Christian Fellowship of the United States of America, founded in 1943, is a fellowship of over 17,000 members of the U.S. Armed Forces, their families and friends. OCF *Emboldens* service men and women in their faith; *Equips* them to be the leaders God has called them to be; *Encourages* them as their faith and profession intersect; and helps them *Engage* with others through their Christian witness and service.

OCF provides opportunities to belong to a family of military believers through Bible study groups; conferences and special programs for marriages, families, children, teens and singles often hosted at our two beautiful conference centers in Colorado and Pennsylvania; fellowship throughout OCF and our social media sites; encouragement and resources through the OCF website; a free subscription to COMMAND magazine; and staff-led ministries near military education centers and the U.S. Service Academies. If you're looking for Christian fellowship at your new duty station, our link-up program can provide you with contacts.

OCF is a charter member of the Evangelical Council for Financial Accountability, Christian Leadership Alliance, Evangelical Press Association, Christian Camp and Conference Association, and Christian Service Charities. OCF is a 501(c)(3) nonprofit organization supported through the gifts of members and friends who want to make an eternal impact in the military and beyond through the ministry of Officers' Christian Fellowship. If you would like to partner with us in this effort, please consider making a donation at www.ocfusa.org/donate. Thank you!

Notes

Notes

Notes